What can psychoanalysis learn from music? What can music learn from psychoanalysis? Can the analysis of music itself provide a primary source of psychological data?

Drawing on Freud's concept of the oral road to the unconscious, *Melodies of the Mind* invites the reader to take a journey on an aural and oral road that explores both music and emotion, and their links to the unconscious. In this book, Julie Jaffee Nagel discusses how musical and psychoanalytic concepts inform each other, showing the ways that music itself provides an exceptional non-verbal pathway to emotion – a source of "quasi" psychoanalytical clinical data. The interdisciplinary synthesis of music and psychoanalytic knowledge provides a schema for understanding the complexity of an individual's inner world as that world interacts with social "reality".

There are three main areas explored:

- The aural road
- Moods and melodies
- The aural/oral road less traveled

Melodies of the Mind is an exploration of the power of music to move us when words fall short. It suggests the value of using music and ideas of the mind to better understand and address psychological, social, and educational issues that are relevant in everyday life. It will be of interest to psychoanalysts, psychologists, music therapists, musicians, music teachers, music students, social workers, educators, professionals in the humanities and social services as well as music lovers.

Julie Jaffee Nagel is a graduate of The Juilliard School, the University of Michigan, and the Michigan Psychoanalytic Institute. She is on the faculty of the Michigan Psychoanalytic Institute and is in private practice in Ann Arbor, Michigan.

Melodies of the Mind

Connections between psychoanalysis and music

Julie Jaffee Nagel

Routledge
Taylor & Francis Group

LONDON AND NEW YORK

First published 2013
by Routledge
27 Church Road, Hove, East Sussex BN3 2FA

Simultaneously published in the USA and Canada
by Routledge
711 Third Avenue, New York, NY 10017

*Routledge is an imprint of the Taylor & Francis Group, an informa
business*

British Library Cataloguing in Publication Data
A catalogue record for this book is available from the British
Library

Library of Congress Cataloging in Publication Data
Nagel, Julie Jaffee.
Melodies of the mind : connections between psychoanalysis and
music / Julie Jaffee Nagel.
p. cm.
Includes bibliographical references.
ISBN 978-0-415-69278-6 (978-0-415-69279-3) 1. Music--
Psychological aspects. 2. Psychoanalysis and music. I. Title.
ML3830.N335 2013
781'.11--dc23
2012022337

ISBN: 978-0-415-69278-6 (hbk)
ISBN: 978-0-415-69279-3 (pbk)
ISBN: 978-0-203-07863-1 (ebk)

Typeset in Garamond
by Saxon Graphics Ltd, Derby

Printed and bound in Great Britain by
TJ International Ltd, Padstow, Cornwall

To Louis, Sonya, David, Sarah, and Rachel
in memory of my mother, Elizabeth Lichtenstein Jaffee, and my
grandparents, Esther and Julian Lichtenstein

Contents

Figures

Foreword

All music lovers – and even some who do not consider themselves music lovers – know that the most direct route to the human soul is through music. A few strains of Bach's Mass in B Minor can bring tears to one's eyes. Music has transported many despairing listeners out of their misery and into a private ecstasy. As the Bard himself informed us, music is also the "food of love." How many lovers have bonded in the context of a particular piece of music that will always be "our song"!

Psychoanalysts might well envy the power of music. The analytic approach is one of carefully and systematically analyzing longstanding defenses against shame and disgust, sitting with silences, and tolerating resistances to looking within. Although patients who come for analytic treatment want help, they are ambivalent about opening up their vulnerable psyches to someone they don't know well, and trusting that the result will be worth the risk. Hence in their own way they put up a bit of a fight when offered understanding by an analyst who is eager to help. If only there were a melody in the toolbox of the analyst – something that would go straight for the heart and melt the defenses of the patient. Alas, psychoanalysts work with the "music" of language, but they must be patient for the kind of emotional responses that musicians take for granted.

Hence on the surface, one would think that the disparate disciplines of music and psychoanalysis might be considered strange bedfellows. However, in this superb melding of these two pursuits, Julie Jaffee Nagel finds areas of overlap, complementarity, and synthesis. Using *fin de siècle* Vienna, where Freud labored to create a new psychoanalytic science, as a stepping-off point, she examines Freud's points of interface with music and musicians. She argues that *classical* psychoanalysis and *classical* music are kindred spirits, perhaps more convergent than divergent.

Psychoanalytic forays into the arts are often categorized as *interdisciplinary psychoanalysis* or *applied psychoanalysis*. Such efforts to bring together psychoanalysis and an art form are often viewed with skepticism because few individuals are sufficiently knowledgeable about both endeavors to craft a convincing synthesis of the two. Often the end result is that an author who is knowledgeable in one of the two disciplines subjugates the other in a sadomasochistic relationship rather than achieving a happy marriage of the two. To our great good fortune, Dr. Nagel is both a psychoanalyst and an accomplished musician trained at Juilliard. She has the rare combination of expertise in two disciplines that make her the ideal person to write this book.

I have followed Dr. Nagel's work for over thirty years. Her keen eye for the disturbances of the psyche was evident in her early interest in the unconscious determinants of stage fright in performers. As she underwent her psychoanalytic training, bravely departing from her original career as a musician, she developed insights into the psychology of music that have broadened our understanding. As she puts it, she studied "how specific formal musical techniques evoke emotional reactions in listeners." Her chapters range widely – from the gangs of juvenile delinquents in Leonard Bernstein's glorious music from *West Side Story,* to Verdi's *Otello.* She appears to be equally facile with both these musical traditions, and she gleans insights from her readers about what moves us when we hear these diverse forms of music.

Dr. Nagel takes a radical stance in her interdisciplinary approach to her dual subjects. She sees the music itself as the psychological data for her study. While most psychoanalysts would look to clinical examples for their inspiration, she departs from this time-honored tradition. The music is quasi-clinical data, the subject of her analytic scrutiny, which she assumes will reveal as much as it conceals for the listener. She eschews "analyzing" the composer to understand the meanings of the music. She goes straight to the source with the assumption that careful attention to the composition itself will tell us what we need to know.

Dr. Nagel is not limited to her deconstruction of music itself. She also ventures into some clinical speculations regarding the unconscious motives of characters in opera. At other times, she provides detailed accounts of actual patients she treated for performance anxiety or other maladies. We see how the psychoanalytic principle of overdetermination or multiple function operates in actual patients and in operatic characters to the same extent. In brief, few emotional conditions are the result of single factors; rather, several converging influences are commonly involved in the pathogenesis of the patient's problems. Dr. Nagel even tells us about her own analysis and how specific music came into her mind, evoking strong feeling and new insights. So many thoughts would rush into her mind simultaneously that she would say to her analyst, "If only I could communicate all of this in music, because I wouldn't be limited to speaking one word at the time." Aside from the underlying dynamics of what she calls her "grandiose wish" to transcend the limitations of speaking with single words, she finds herself in agreement with Susanne Langer's view that music has the capacity to express more fully the ambivalence of human beings about their desires and their fears.

Throughout this volume, the reader is challenged to think outside the box regarding the influence of music on psychoanalysis and vice versa. Dr. Nagel takes us on a musical journey that haunts us but enlightens us at the same time. We cannot know or articulate the far-ranging impact of music on our collective psyche. But we experience the rush of excitement, the flooding of tears, and the almost transcendent experience that music brings to our day-to-day, humdrum routines. I suggest that you take this ride with Dr. Nagel, and let the sounds lift your spirit and enlighten your mind. You won't regret it.

Glen O. Gabbard

Preface

Melodies in my mind have been evolving for a long time. My book *Melodies of the Mind* synthesizes musical and psychoanalytic concepts in my examination of the nonverbal qualities of *music itself*, which have the potential to evoke meaningful emotional experiences for the listener. My leitmotif in each chapter is that the formal qualities of music, used illustratively as psychological "data" in specific examples, and psychoanalytic principles mutually inform each other. This blending of musical and psychoanalytic knowledge provides an elegant schema for understanding the complexity of affects and their function as unique, nonverbal pathways into unconscious processes, integral to clinical work. Interdisciplinary exploration also serves as a model for examining the value and uses of music and psychoanalytic knowledge, both within and beyond the consulting room and the concert hall.

The opening chapter of *Melodies of the Mind* invites the reader to consider the power and relevance of music in mental life and includes a survey of psychoanalytic writings from a historical perspective. Although in the past ten to fifteen years, there have been a number of books written about music, emotion, and meaning from various theoretical perspectives, my focus will be upon classical psychoanalytic literature pertaining to music. In particular, I will examine changes in psychoanalytic thinking regarding the significance of music in mental life, a topic that fascinates and challenges those who tackle it from any theoretical perspective. My approach will delineate specific parameters in classical psychoanalytic theory and particular classical music concepts as springboards to illustrate how specific formal musical techniques evoke emotional reactions in listeners. Each chapter presents a "case-ette" – a metaphorical amalgamation of clinical vignettes and musical compositions.

Music has unique formal properties – its own language – i.e., melody, rhythm, pitch, tonality, form, dynamics, which have specific meaning. Certain musical concepts such as modulation, enharmonic, consonance, dissonance, tension, ambiguity, and so on overlap with the process and content inherent in psychoanalytic theory and practice. The latter includes multiple function, overdetermination, displacement, dissonance, consonance, silence, tension, conflict, and ambiguity. My approach to understanding emotion and music does not focus upon a composer's possible motivations that may underlie his or her writing or the performer's creativity, important as these topics are. Rather, I emphasize that music is the auditory representational world of all individuals. Probing the symbols and structures of music has the potential to contribute to a deeper understanding of mental life.

Similarly, psychodynamic principles will be presented in a manner that highlights their overlap with the formal structures of classical music. *Fin de siecle* Vienna serves both as the musical and the psychoanalytic milieu to anchor my preamble as a verbal prelude to the case-ettes that follow. We will see that it was in this city and at this time that Sigmund Freud was developing his theory and technique of psychoanalysis, at the same time that traditional tonal structures of the Romantic period were dissolved in the hands of composers such as Arnold Schoenberg, Alban Berg, and Anton Webern.

Part I begins the expedition. I consider the idea that "music is the analogue of emotional life" (Feder, 2004, p. 3). What does music convey? What does it represent? How does it do so? What can psychoanalysis learn from music? What can music learn from psychoanalysis?

Freud balked at the suggestion that he himself appreciated music, claiming he was tone deaf. Freud's antipathy toward music, despite his living and working in tumultuous *fin de siècle* Vienna, will be explored. We will examine his close relationship with Max Graf, noted musicologist and member of his inner circle, who used Freud's psychoanalytic theories to explicate music. Graf was also the father – and the analyst! – of Herbert Graf (whom Freud called "Little Hans" in his clinical description of the case), who was to become the stage manager at the Metropolitan Opera in New York in 1936. I will suggest that, during this time, the oral road of dreams and the aural road of music diverged, or at least detoured, as pathways to the unconscious.

My preamble introduces the concepts of multiple function, displacement, and multiple representation, which are shared by both music and psychoanalytic theory. These concepts, the bedrock of Freud's *The Interpretation of Dreams* (1900), symbolically cross the boundaries of each discipline's individual and unique theoretical canons, adding depth and breadth to both. Pertinent psychoanalytic and musical literature will be reviewed to illustrate that, despite music's lack of Freud's benediction, scholars have continued to pursue connections between music, mind, and meaning in the decades since his death. Music with and without verbal texts will be analyzed. My polemic emphasizes that the functions and formal structures of music and of psychoanalysis are overdetermined, have multiple functions, and are infinitely displaceable. Rather than *divergence,* there is a *convergence* between them.

Part II consists of six case-ettes, each exploring various affects and ideas evoked by specific musical themes and compositional techniques. In the first case-ette, "Ambiguity – The Tritone in 'Gee, Officer Krupke' from *West Side Story,*" I will point out that the dissonant musical interval of the *tritone,* which historically and harmonically represents instability, is heard throughout

Leonard Bernstein's rich musical score. It evokes intrapsychic, interpersonal, affective, and social dramas that unfold within and between two ethnically-based gangs, the Puerto Rican Sharks and the Caucasian Jets. I give particular emphasis to an overtly comic song with serious underpinnings, "Gee, Officer Krupke." Bernstein's sensitivity to the ambiguity and tension inherent in the tritone and his masterful use of it in *West Side Story* are conceptualized as an intersection of musical theory and theories of the mind.

I discuss Sergei Prokofiev's 1936 musical fairy tale *Peter and the Wolf* and its incorporation of musical and psychoanalytic functions in case-ette 2. In particular, I focus on the use of instrumentation and orchestration to illustrate the coming of age of the protagonist, Peter – his intrapsychic transformation and the consolidation of his self-esteem as he ventures beyond his grandfather's garden and captures the wolf. The composer's management of the musical material and his highlighting of the metaphorical meanings inherent in the animal characters extend beyond usual compositional technique; all the animals are seen to be present within Peter, and indeed as residing within the human psyche.

My focus on Mozart in case-ette 3 centers upon the composer's musical compositions and the psychological impact of his mother's death in 1778 – the year when mother and son traveled to Paris together without Mozart's father, Leopold. In the summer of 1778, at the age of twenty-two, Mozart composed his piano sonata in A Minor, K. 310, which is the musical/psychological focus of this case-ette. Marked by a sense of gravity and by its departure from both Mozart's own and others' compositional styles, this unique work draws attention to the distinctive yet elusive representation of affect through the nonverbal medium of music, the medium in which the composer stated that he best expressed himself.

In my discussion of Verdi's *Otello*, I will isolate the composer's choices regarding specific key centers in the "Bacio" ("Kiss") theme in order to illustrate particular harmonic musical techniques that evoke emotional responses. Formal tonal relationships establish dramatic associations and mental schemas. Tonality "works" to make this opera aurally and technically cohesive, powerful, and expressive. Thus, two particular tonal centers are emphasized as sonic psychic representations and compromise formations expressed in sound. As listeners, we become caught up in a musical and dramatic, transformative experience, as we experience Otello's jealousy and *hear* a kiss of love become a kiss of death.

In case-ette 5, psychoanalysis and music are synthesized, with an emphasis on the origins and vicissitudes of shame and guilt as seen in the emotional disintegration of Lucia in Donizetti's opera *Lucia di Lammermoor*. Lucia's affects and her intrapsychic and interpersonal dynamics are heard in the *bel canto* style of the music itself. Musical examples, especially Lucia's "Mad Scene," illustrate particular psychological concepts pertinent to the affects of guilt and shame.

The polyphonic, or multiple, functions of music enable us to feel both elevating and disquieting dynamics simultaneously. Experiencing contrasting/conflicting emotions concurrently through music is distinct from verbal discourse, which allows for expression of only one word at a time. During "The Tonight Ensemble," discussed in case-ette 6, each character and the two gangs in *West Side Story* sing in various tonalities and rhythms. Individually and then all together, they express their hopes, dreams, fears, conflicts, and anxieties through the music. The "Tonight Ensemble" is a sophisticated blend of sonic polyphony and psychoanalytic principles. Its formal balance of multiple musical elements resonates with the disparities among simultaneously conflicting impulses, defenses, affects, and actions that we all experience.

It is no longer necessary, if it ever was, to think of applied – or interdisciplinary – psychoanalysis as the "unruly stepchild of clinical orthodoxy" (Feder, 1993, p. 3). The serious study of music from an analytic perspective is at once intrapsychic and interpersonal, conscious and unconscious. Interdisciplinary studies have the potential to reach an audience beyond the clinical choir. The overdetermined sonic potentials of music can create aural relationships between music and psychoanalytic ideas and between listener and music. My final chapter, "The Aural/Oral Road Less Traveled," emphasizes the importance and vitality of future directions along the path where music and psychoanalysis intertwine.

Melodies of the Mind is intended for readers who are curious about a creative interdisciplinary synergy and broad application of ideas. Both psychoanalysts and musicians can play a leadership role in addressing community and social issues in the twenty-first century. The concepts that link music with psychoanalysis and tone with talk have practical implications for cross-pollination in formulating how we tune into and are moved by what we hear. The formal properties of music and psychoanalytic concepts provide a vibrant point of intersection among music theory and theories of mind, one that holds implications for clinical practice and musical performance, and that can transport music and psychoanalytic concepts into the community, beyond the walls of each individual discipline. This larger community includes partnerships with education, cultural institutions, humanities programs, social service agencies, social media, mental health organizations, music teachers, performers, music students and music lovers. I invite you to join me on a journey on oral and aural roads that includes – but also extends beyond – the consulting room and the concert hall.

Acknowledgments

To acknowledge those people who have made contributions to my life and my professional development offers an opportunity for reflection. The people to whom I offer appreciation came into my life at different times and in various ways. All have contributed to my personal and professional journey through musical and psychoanalytic landscapes. All have contributed to the melodies in my mind.

The late Stephen Paledes, my piano teacher in Newport News, Virginia, encouraged and prepared me to attend The Juilliard School, which proved to be a momentous turning point in my life. Jerry Lowder, my high school choir teacher at Newport News High School, wisely advised me to "keep my options open" as I entered The Juilliard School, also momentous in retrospect. Years later, Jesse Gordon nourished my hybrid interests and Edward Bordin influenced my career redirection as my doctoral advisors at The University of Michigan. Howard Shevrin, as my clinical supervisor, encouraged my interest in music and mind during my postdoctoral work at the University of Michigan. I appreciate Owen Renik's confidence in me when he urged me to present a paper at the Meetings of The American Psychoanalytic Association when I was a first year Candidate at the Michigan Psychoanalytic Institute.

My appreciation is extended to the Center for the Education of Women at The University of Michigan, which supported my academic interests in my second career.

For over thirty years, Glen Gabbard has been an inspiring mentor, generous colleague, and unwavering, cherished friend. I value his tremendous influence on my career. The late Stuart Feder's enthusiasm for conceptualizing music as a point of entry into affect and unconscious processes inspired me to consider music as nonverbal psychoanalytic/clinical data. He was a treasured friend, colleague, and mentor; his presence is felt throughout this book.

I have met Pinchas Noy only through his extraordinary writings on music and emotion and through our email exchanges between Israel and the United States. His pioneering work in music and emotion has had a major impact on my analytic and musical thinking. Peter Lowenberg has generously fostered my interdisciplinary ideas. I also have been fortunate to find support for many years from Salman Akhtar, who encouraged me to write with imagination. I have shared many creative and meaningful conversations with Laurie Wilson, my co-chair of the American Psychoanalytic Association Committee on Arts and Psychoanalysis.

Amica mia Gina Atkinson has been invaluable in helping me edit early drafts of this book. Her patience, extraordinary professional skills, and exquisite sensitivity both to words and music are represented on every page.

Mark Eden Horowitz, senior music specialist at the Library of Congress, has assisted immeasurably in researching scores, particularly those of Leonard Bernstein.

My colleagues at the Michigan Psychoanalytic Institute and The American Psychoanalytic Association have provided analytic homes in which many of my ideas took shape. In particular, Charles Burch has been selflessly available to discuss the complexities of inner life. Linda Brakel's research in primary process and a-rational thought has expanded my ideas. Channing Lipson helped me discover my analytic voice while sharing a mutual interest in music. Elsa Poole and Diane Hammer at the New Orleans-Birmingham Psychoanalytic Center have offered encouragement and opportunities to present my work.

Riccardo Lombardi, my colleague and friend in Rome, Italy, has deepened my understanding about the relationship between body and mind as it pertains to music.

Melvin Lansky and Stanley Coen have encouraged me to think outside the box; my ideas have been motivated frequently by theirs. Roy Schafer, a new friend but someone I "have known" for many years through his writing, has been an inspiration for the analytic attitude that I attempt to bring to my work.

Throughout the variety of feelings I have experienced in writing this book, I have valued the integrity of my analyst, Peter Blos, Jr.. Our analytic collaboration allowed me to discover new meanings in my old melodies and enrich my emotional repertoire.

I would like to thank Kate Hawes, Kirsten Buchanan, Rob Brown, Kelly Landers, Rachel Norridge and Natalie Meylan at Routledge Press for their support and keen editorial observations in bringing this book to publication.

My appreciation is extended to the following publishers who have given permission to use my previous work and musical examples in this book: *Journal of the American Psychoanalytic Association* (Sage Publications), *Psychoanalytic Quarterly*, *American Imago* (John Hopkins University Press), *The Bulletin of the Menninger Clinic* (Guilford Press), and Boosey & Hawkes. Please see below for full credit line and permissions information:

Guilford Press for permission to use adapted material from Nagel, J. J. (1998). Injury and Pain in Performing Musicians: A Psychodynamic Perspective, *Bulletin of the Menninger Clinic*, 62 (1), Winter: 85–93. Copyright Guilford Press. Reprinted with permission of the Guilford Press.

Boosey & Hawkes, Inc. for permission to use excerpts from *Tonight – Ensemble* by Leonard Bernstein, words by Stephen Sondheim © Copyright 1956, 1957, 1958, 1959 by Amberson Holdings LLC and Stephen Sondheim. Copyright renewed. Leonard Bernstein Music Publishing Company LLC, publisher. Boosey & Hawkes, agent for rental. International copyright secured. Reprinted with permission.

Boosey & Hawkes, Inc. for permission to use excerpts from "Gee, Officer Krupke" by Leonard Bernstein, words by Stephen Sondheim © Copyright 1956, 1957, 1958, 1959 by Amberson Holdings LLC and Stephen Sondheim. Copyright renewed. Leonard Bernstein Music Publishing Company LLC, publisher. Boosey & Hawkes, agent for rental. International copyright secured. Reprinted by permission.

The Psychoanalytic Quarterly for permission to use "Psychoanalytic Perspectives on Music: An Intersection on the Oral and Aural Road." First published in © *The Psychoanalytic Quarterly*, 2008, 77 (2): 507–30.

Johns Hopkins University Press, Copyright © 2007 The Johns Hopkins University Press. This article, "Melodies of the Mind: Mozart in 1778," first appeared in *American Imago,* 64 (1) (2007): 23–36. Reprinted with permission by The Johns Hopkins University Press.

Thanks also to Sage Publications Inc.'s permission to use the following material:

Nagel, J. J. (2010). Psychoanalytic and Musical Ambiguity: The Tritone in "Gee, Officer Krupke", *Journal of the American Psychoanalytic Association*, 58 (1): 9-25.

Nagel, J. J. (2008). Psychoanalytic and Musical Perspectives on Shame in Donizetti's *Lucia di Lammermoor, Journal of the American Psychoanalytic Association*, 56 (2): 551–63.

Every effort has been made to obtain permission from International Universities Press to use part of the article, Nagel, J. J., Music, Animals, and Psychoanalysis, in *The Cultural Zoo,* edited by S. Akhtar and V. Volkan (2005). Permission has been granted by S. Akhtar and V. Volkan (eds) to use adapted material from "Music, Animals, and Psychoanalysis" in this book.

My earliest ventures into music were nurtured lovingly by my late mother, Elizabeth Lichtenstein Jaffee and my grandparents, Esther and Julian Lichtenstein. My husband, Louis' extraordinary musicianship and companionship as well as his support and encouragement have been part of my life since our Juilliard days and especially during the rigors of writing this book; my talented and caring daughter, Sonya; my son-in-law, David; and my two granddaughters, Sarah and Rachel, bring beautiful music, vibrant energy, and limitless pleasure into my life. I dedicate my book to all of them.

Discography

Selected CDs and DVDs for music cited in case-ettes

Case-ettes 1 and 6

Leonard Bernstein: **West Side Story**

DVD

Bernstein, L., Sondheim, S., Laurents, A. and Robbins, J. (1961). *West Side Story*, Metro-Goldwyn-Mayer Studios, Inc.

The Making of West Side Story – Kiri Te Kanawa, Jose Carreras, Tatiana Troyanos, Kurt Ollmann. Conducted by Leonard Bernstein.

CD

Bernstein, L., Sondheim, S., Laurents, A., and Robbins, J. (1957). *West Side Story* (original Broadway cast recording), Columbia Broadway Masterworks, Sony Classical.

Case-ette 2

Sergei Prokofiev: **Peter and the Wolf**

CD

Peter and the Wolf – Leonard Bernstein, New York Philharmonic (narrated by Mr. Bernstein). Saint-Saens: Carnival of the Animals (Columbia Masterworks)

Children's Classics – Prokofiev: *Peter and the Wolf*/Saint Saens: *Carnival of the Animals*/Britten: *Young Person's Guide to the Orchestra* (Bernstein Century). New York Philharmonic Orchestra (Sony Classical).

Prokofiev: *Peter and the Wolf*, Mari Rossi, Wiener Staatsopernorchester, Boris Karloff, Narrator (Vanguard Classics).

Sergei Prokofiev: *Peter and the Wolf*; Jean-Pascal Benitus: Wolf Tracks, Russian National Orchestra, Kent Nagano – Mikhail Gorbachev, Sophia Loren, Bill Clinton, Narrators.

Case-ette 3

W. A. Mozart: Sonata in A Minor, K. 310

CD

Piano Sonatas K. 310, K.331, K.533/494 – Murray Perahia (Sony Classics).

Piano Sonatas K.310, K.331, K. 332, Fantasia in D Minor – Mitsuko Uchida (Philips).

Klaviersonaten Piano Sonatas Vol. 3 – K. 309, K.310, K. 311, K. 331 – Alicia de Larrocha (RCA Victor).

The Complete Piano Sonatas and Variations – Daniel Barenboim (EMI Classics).

The Piano Sonatas (Box Set) – Andras Schiff (London).

Piano Sonatas K. 310, K. 311 K. 533/494, Fantasy K. 397 – Alfred Brendel (Philips).

Piano Sonatas K. 281, K. 310, Variations K. 398/Fantasie K. 397 – Emil Gliels (Deutsche Grammophon).

The Piano Sonatas, Vol. I – Glen Gould (Odyssey).

Bach, Mozart, Scarlatti, Schubert – Dinu Lipatti (EMI Classics).

Case-ette 4

Giuseppi Verdi: Otello

DVD

Otello – Placido Comingo, Renee Fleming, James Morris. Metropolitan Opera Orchestra and Chorus/James Levine (Deutche Grammophon).

Otello – Jon Vickers, Renata Scotto, Cornell MacNeil. Metropolitan Opera Orchestra and Chorus/James Levine (Sony).

Otello – Placido Domingo, Kiri Te Kanawa, Sergi Leiferkus. The Royal Opera/ Covent Garden/Georg Solti (Kultur).

CD

Otello – Placido Domingo, Renee Fleming, James Morris. Metropolitan Opera Orchestra and Chorus/James Levine (Deutsche Grammophon).

Otello – Placido Domingo, Renata Scotto, Sherrill Milnes. National Philharmonic Orchestra/James Levine (The RCA Opera Treasury).

Otello – Jon Vickers, Mirella Freni, Peter Glossop. Berliner Philharmoiker/ Herbert Von Karajan (EMI Classics).

Case-ette 5

Gaetano Donizetti: Lucia di Lammermoor

DVD

Lucia di Lammermoor – Anna Netrebko, Piotr Beczala, Mariusz Kwiecien, Ildar Abdrazakov. Metropolitan Opera/Marco Armiliato (Deutche Grammophon).

Lucia di Lammermoor – Joan Sutherland, Alfredo Kraus, Pablo Elvira, Paul Plishka. Metropolitan Opera /Richard Bonynge (Deutsche Grammophon).

Lucia di Lammermoor – Natalie Dessay, Piotr Beczala, Ilya Bannik, Vladislav Sulimsky. Marinsky Orchestra/Valery Gergiev.

CD

Lucia di Lammermoor – Complete Opera (with full libretto and translation). Beverly Sills, Carol Bergonzi, Piero Cappuccilli, Justino Diaz. London Symphony Orchestra/Thomas Schippers (Westminster).

Lucia di Lammermoor – Complete Opera. Maria Callas, Tito Gobbi, Guiseppe di Stefano, Raffaele Arie. Orchestra e Coro del Maggio Musicale Fiorentino/ Tullio Serafin (EMI Classics).

Lucia di Lammermoor – Joan Sutherland, Luciano Pavarotti, Sherill Milnes, Nicolai Ghiaurov. Chorus and Orchestra of the Royal Opera House, Covent Garden/Richard Boynge (Decca).

Part I

The aural road

Chapter I

Preamble

Music has affected me deeply and differently at various times in my life. I believe my attraction to the piano at a very young age and my immersion in music professionally were unconscious motivations that decades later contributed to my appreciation of the depth, elegance, and musicality of psychoanalytic ideas. Trained both as a musician and a psychoanalyst, I am interested in my own internal life, the emotional lives of others, as well as the inner workings of music. Particularly during my psychoanalytic training, I became curious about what resonated in me when words had limited value.

Why, for example, did Leonard Bernstein's "Age of Anxiety" comfort me immediately following the heartbreaking, untimely death of my mother? Why did I gravitate to the piano at the age of four and pursue it seriously as a career for many years? Why do I continue to be fascinated with music and, like a magnet, drawn to its intersection with affect? What was it about classical music that attracted me as an adolescent, especially when all my friends were enamored with the top ten songs of the week (although I listened to them as well, I unabashedly admit, as I navigated my teen years and my musical ambitions).

For as long as I can remember, I have always felt a resonance and a romance with "serious" music because it has provided comfort, assuaged sadness, made me feel happy, joyful, strong, and sometimes evoked a melancholy I did not understand and could not express verbally. I am now more aware of how much music helped me feel what I could not articulate. I have come to realize how music served as my companion at a time of loss and at joyous moments. I believe that one "thinks" as well as feels in music (Lipson, 2006). Music can also function as an aural transitional object, like a child's teddy bear or beloved blankie, to provide comfort when mother – or father – is not available, either physically or emotionally (McDonald, 1970). Clearly, this was the case for me and, as I have seen over many years in my clinical practice, has been so for many of my patients. Out of sight is neither out of mind nor out of earshot. I feel attuned to Pratt's (1952) proposal that "music sounds the way emotion feels" (cited in Feder et al., 1993, p. 127) and to Feder's (unpublished) belief that music, in addition to a composer's underlying motivations for expressing him or herself through an aural pathway, has the capacity to represent a "psychic semblance of inner life."

Realizing there are multiple and differing implications for composer, performer, and listener (and for those who think and write about music and emotion), I emphasize in the pages that follow that a listener's affects and psychic processes can be evoked through music, an abstract sound-language comprised of notation, rhythm, and formal qualities, which provides a unique aural entry into mental life.

Music can provide accompaniment as well as accompany and enhance important life events such as weddings, funerals, parties, and official ceremonies. It enhances the mood in movies and is played as background noise, in varying decibels, in places such as restaurants, department or grocery stores, coffee shops, hotel lobbies, and elevators. The concert hall does not hold a monopoly on music in our lives. Music has been used as propaganda to promote or suppress political ideology, such as occurred under Stalin's dictatorship and in Nazi Germany. Music can embellish or represent a programmed story (e.g., Strauss's tone poems, "Til Eulenspiegel," *Don Juan*, "Ein Heldenleben"; J. S. Bach's "Capriccio on the Departure of a Beloved Brother"; Robert Schumann's "Kreisleriana," "Papillons"; and Dukas's "Sorcerer's Apprentice"), demonstrate and/or be inspired by a mood (e.g., Beethoven's *Pastoral Symphony*, Debussy's *Three Nocturnes*: "Nuages," "Fetes," and "Sirnes," and Ravel's "Jeux d'eau"), sonically illustrate a narrative (e.g., St. Saens's *Carnival of the Animals,* Prokofieff's *Peter and the Wolf,* Britten's *Young Person's Guide to the Orchestra*), and/or be combined with words, as in musical theater and opera. Regarding the latter categories, the words, the libretti, and prearranged narratives add ideational and/or verbal text to music and allow for additional oral and, in the case of opera or musical theater, visual pathways to unconscious processes. Yet *music itself* – without words or programmatic specificities – can significantly influence the listener's capacity to feel, to access affects that otherwise may be verbally inexpressible and/or emotionally unavailable.

Thus, the analysis of *music itself* as a primary source of psychological data is the distinctive method of analysis that I bring to my interdisciplinary exploration of mental processes and affect. In the chapters that follow, *music itself* will serve as the "quasi" clinical data, although I will also include clinical vignettes to illustrate both psychoanalytic and musical concepts. My approach is distinct from examining an individual's emotional response to music, to the biographical background of a composer, to cultural milieu, to psychopathology, and to the mysteries of creativity, although all of these factors are embedded to some degree in how I conceptualize music as an aural pathway to emotion and unconscious processes.

The parameters in the chapters that follow, called *case-ettes,* are organized around a blend of oral and aural aspects of clinical vignettes and specific music compositions. I have chosen to initiate the journey by exploring aspects of classical Freudian theory and classical Western musical tradition. The tumultuous and fertile cultural soil of *fin de siècle* Vienna serves as a backdrop and launch. My parameters, which both facilitate and limit my analytic/ musical range, are a function of my hybrid training in music and psychoanalysis, my fascination with Freud's disclaimers about music, the breakdown of tonal music, and the divergence and subsequent convergence of interest in music and mental life. Clearly, other psychoanalytic and musical perspectives not explored here also hold relevance for the examination of music as a point of entry into affect and unconscious processes.

With the aim of raising more questions than I can answer and encouraging cross-pollination among scholars, mental health professionals, musicologists, and music lovers, the chapters that follow explore the following overdetermined themes:

• Music and psychoanalytic concepts hold enduring value as each informs and enriches the other.
• Music serves as an important entry into affect and unconscious processes.
• Music and psychoanalytic principles are relevant both inside and beyond the concert hall and consulting room and contribute to a nuanced understanding of our contemporary educational, cultural, and social milieu.

The oral/aural road diverges

By the time Freud was immersed in developing classical psychoanalytic theory, music theory and performance practice had already claimed a history. Living and working in *fin de siècle* Vienna, Freud was in the midst of his discoveries about the mind as the musical tonality and harmonic vocabulary of the late Romantic period of music history were being stretched aurally and theoretically by composers such as Wagner, Strauss, and Mahler, eventually breaking down altogether into atonality.

Die Traumdeutung (*The Interpretation of Dreams*), regarded by Freud as his most important work, made its debut in 1899, although the title page is dated 1900. In his two-part Dream Books (*S. E.,* Vols IV and V), which sold only 351 copies in the six years following publication (Freud, 1953, *S. E.,* Vol. IV, p. xx), Freud laid the foundation for a psychology of the mind based on psychic energies as distinct from purely neurophysiological/anatomical perspectives. In his own words in the preface to the first edition, "I have attempted in this volume to give an account of the interpretation of dreams; and in doing so I have not, I believe, trespassed beyond the sphere of interest covered by neuro-pathology" (Freud, *S. E.,* Vol. IV, p. xxiii).

Freud famously labeled dreams the "royal road to a knowledge of the unconscious activities of the mind" (1900, p. 608). His leap from soma to psyche bequeathed enormous innovations for theoretical and clinical perspectives regarding mental processes: symbolic functions, manifest and latent contents, multiple determinants, displacements, and, importantly, primary and secondary processes in mental functioning. Freud's formulations about the unconscious, free association, the linkage of overtly opposing mental contents and affects, and primary and secondary processes are compatible symbolically with the concepts that I will explore in regard to selected musical paradigms. While musical innovation and psychoanalysis germinated in the same creative sociocultural soil, they subsequently diverged on oral and aural roads to the unconscious.

To give a historical anchor and a tonal orientation, in the Classical period in Western music (spanning the years approximately 1740–1800), specific rules of tonal/harmonic organization were arranged around the eight-note diatonic scale. Familiar composers from the Classical period include Franz Josef Hayden, Carl Philipp Emanuel Bach, Wolfgang Amadeus Mozart, and Ludwig van Beethoven, whose music formed a bridge to the Romantic period that followed. These composers utilized a system that dictated the resolution of harmonies to a tonic, or home, key. This was not only an expectation of a predictable compositional procedure, but also a matter of the listener's anticipation. Dissonance or modulation away from the home key was always followed by a return to the tonic (the home key), producing a sense of completion, satisfaction, rest, and finality. Here one might think analytically in terms of tension/release, unpleasure/pleasure, and musically of dissonance/consonance. Further, the tones in the diatonic scale had *un*equal power (whole and half-tones), which contributed to tonal and aural expectations regarding resolution of harmonies.

Chronologically, the era in music history that emerged from the Classical period is known as the Romantic period (approximately 1800–1890) – although, as noted by Grout and Palisca (1996), there is more continuity than contrast in harmonic vocabulary and conventions of rhythm and form when moving from one era to the next. Differences in style were typically observed "by degree" (Grout and Palisca, 1996, p. 563). In the world of "ordered sound" (p. 564) that does not represent a concrete world, Romantic music was believed to evoke mental impressions and intense affects. Philosopher Arthur Schopenhauer (1788–1860) maintained that "music was the incarnation of the innermost reality, the immediate expression of universal feelings and impulses in concrete, definite form" (cited in Grout and Palisca, 1996, p. 564).

Some thought that music of the Romantic era, particularly music without words, communicated pure emotion. Additionally, the *art song,* or *lied,* steeped in the words of poetry and literature, occupied a major place in the Romantic literature. Composers such as Franz Schubert, Robert Schumann, Hugo Wolf, and Johannes Brahms developed this genre, elegantly uniting words and music. Purely instrumental, programmatic music emerged in the form of the *tone poem,* made popular by composers such as Franz Liszt, its inventor, and Richard Strauss. In this context, music without words was inspired by stories that were aurally depicted in compositional form.

The late Romantic period is known harmonically by its movement toward *chromaticism*, although at first, the music representative of this departure from traditional tonal centers typically resolved to the expected tonic. Of importance was the growing tendency for key/tonal centers, easily identifiable through expected harmonies in the Classical and early Romantic periods, to become increasingly ambiguous; expected harmonic resolutions were delayed and eventually became unclear. What *is* clear is that in the late 1800s there was a stretching of the boundaries of tonality and movement away from earlier theoretical harmonic canons. The late Romantic, chromatic style was exemplified by the work of composers such as Richard Wagner (who flourished in the mid-nineteenth century and died in 1883), Gustav Mahler, Richard Strauss, and Alexander Scriabin.

The ambiguous opening chord of the prelude to Wagner's opera *Tristan and Isolde* is perhaps more widely discussed than any other chord in musical history. The unexpected nature of its harmony, both literally and symbolically, is resolved many hours later, and only at the conclusion of the "Liebestod" at the end of the opera. Freud would have been nine years old at the time of Wagner's historical musical premier, which to many music historians marks the irreversible onset of tonal disintegration.

The "Tristan Chord," and indeed the entire opera *Tristan and Isolde,* symbolized the period of musical history in Vienna that found its most revolutionary representative in composer Arnold Schoenberg (1874–1951), the architect of atonal and twelve-tone music. *Atonal* music has no tonal center and departs from the traditional treatment of harmony. *Serial* music is based on the composition of a row or series "consisting of twelve tones or pitch classes of the octave arranged in an order the composer chooses" (Grout and Palisca, 1996, p. 736). These twelve pitches may be used melodically, harmonically, rhythmically, or intervalically (forward, backward, and/or inverted upside down), in any way the composer chooses. All twelve tones are used before the composer uses any single note for a second time. This non-redundancy "implies that the relative positions within the series must be respected" (Rosen, 1996, p. 84).

Twelve-tone music, however, is not necessarily atonal and therefore could potentially have a tonal center. Schoenberg's compositional inventions have been labeled *the democracy of tones* since all notes of the octave are treated equally – i.e., each pitch is as important as every other. The major impact of Schoenberg's technique was that tonality and harmony, as they had been known for centuries, were dissolved as structural organizers. Harmony ceased to have its conventional function (i.e., dissonant chords no longer resolved consonantly). One writer suggested that Schoenberg tried to dissolve music altogether (Botstein, 1999, p. 41).

Thinking psychoanalytically, the equality of the twelve tones produced in any order may be likened to free association, just as the tonal uncertainty in the "Tristan chord" shares an aural connection to the psychoanalytic concept of ambiguity and mental conflict.

In his *Theory of Harmony*, Schoenberg wrote, "Inside where the man of instinct begins, there, fortunately, all theory breaks down" (*Harmonielehre*, 1911, p. 449–50). Approximately one year earlier, he had commented:

> Art is a cry of distress from those who live out within themselves the destiny of humanity .... They are those who do not turn their eyes away to protect themselves from emotions but open them wide to oppose what must be attacked. They do, however, often close their eyes to perceive what the senses do not convey, to look inside of what seems to be happening on the surface. Inside them turns the movement of the world; only an echo of it leaks out – the work of art.
>
> ("Aphorismen", 1910, in Arnold Schoenberg, "Schopferische Konfessionem", ed. Willi Reich, (Zurich, 1964), p. 12.)

Both this new system of musical expression and the development of psychoanalysis were traveling into uncharted regions along parallel oral and aural paths. The two did not intersect.

In his string sextet *Verklarte Nacht (Transfigured Night)*, composed in 1899 (the same year in which Freud published *The Interpretation of Dreams*) when Schoenberg was twenty-five, the composer stretched tonality almost to its breaking point while continuing to use traditional chromaticism. It was, by 1890s' standards, hardly revolutionary, yet it created controversy. A contemporary commented, "It sounds as if someone had smeared the score of 'Tristan' while it was still wet" (Rosen, 1996, p. 3). A music society in Vienna refused to allow its performance, ostensibly because it contained one dissonance that had yet to be classified in any textbook.

After 1908, moral outrage began to be expressed by the public over Schoenberg's work. An outright riot ensued after a concert in 1913 – a riot reported to have surpassed the notorious uproar in Paris after the first performance of Stravinsky's *Rite of Spring*. (It is perhaps unnecessary to observe here that music aroused strong affect.) Although there was public displeasure over Schoenberg's Chamber Symphony No. 1, Op. 9, it was the song cycle written by his pupil Alban Berg, *Altenberg Lieder*, that forced the program to be canceled and the police called. Charles Rosen commented:

> Stylistic revolutions of those years were merely the exploitation of already existent possibilities within the artistic languages .... The sense of rebellion cannot be easily dismissed. Much of the music and art of that period is deliberately provocative and expresses a defiance, even a profound horror, of the society in which the artists lived .... The normally difficult relation between artist and public [became] a pathological one .... The artist's answer to ideological pressure was one of deliberate provocation, while the public came to believe that a violent response to such provocation was a citizen's right and even a patriotic duty.
>
> (1996, p. 8)

During Schoenberg's pre-atonal period, Freud wrote *The Interpretation of Dreams* (1899/1900), *The Psychopathology of Everyday Life* (1901), "Fragment of an Analysis of a Case of Hysteria" (1905), and *Three Essays on the Theory of Sexuality* (1905).

By 1909, however, Schoenberg's break with earlier musical style – including his own – was almost complete with *Ewartung* (*Awaiting* or *Expectation*). It was written in just seventeen days, between August 27 and September 12, 1909. The text was authored by Marie Pappenheim, a twenty-seven-year-old medical student in Vienna and a member of Schoenberg's inner circle. The psychodrama behind *Ewartung* is a series of disjointed sentences uttered by a woman as she wanders through the forest at night, looking for her lover. The lack of linear musical development could be seen as representing her stream of consciousness.

Written at the time Schoenberg had been abandoned by his wife for his best friend, the topic and text suggest an autobiographical edge of alienation, depression, and inner disintegration. Personally distraught and publicly criticized for his work, Schoenberg was considering suicide.

1909 was the year Freud published "Analysis of a Phobia in a Five-Year-Old Boy ('Little Hans')" and "Notes Upon a Case of Obsessional Neurosis" (in which he described his patient known as the Rat Man).

Another nocturnal theme is set forth in *Pierrot Lunaire*, composed in 1912, three years after *Ewartung*. (Between 1911 and 1915, Freud wrote "Psycho-Analytic Notes on an Autobiographical Account of a Case of Paranoia [Dementia Paranoides]," in which he described the case history of Schreber, and his *Papers on Technique*.) Written between March 12 and May 30, it was first performed on October 16, 1912, in a small theater in Berlin, with Schoenberg conducting. The composer wrote: "The sounds are starting to express physical and psychological impulses of literally animal-like immediacy" (Schoenberg, *Berlin Diary*, in record notes for *Pierrot Lunaire*, p. 7, Teldec, 1997).

Furthermore, Schoenberg gives us clues to his creative impulse in his subsequent writing about *Pierrot Lunaire*. His ideas feel inordinately close to the evolving psychoanalytic concepts of free association, primary and secondary process, overdeterminism, and multiple function as he observes:

> It is impossible for a person to feel only one thing at a time …. This lack of logic that our feelings reveal, this lack of logic demonstrated by the associations revealed by a rising wave of blood or by some physical or nervous reaction – it is this that I should like to have in my music.
>
> (*Pierrot Lunaire* jacket notes, Teldec, 1997, p. 9)

In this work, Pierrot expresses himself as a moonbeam and imagines a gruesome fantasy in which giant bats trap him and shut out the sun. Schoenberg utilizes twenty-one poems by Albert Giraud, which are organized into three groups of seven. The second group is filled with hallucinations about killings. For example, song #11 is entitled "Red Mass"; here Pierrot climbs onto an altar and shows "his own heart, in bloody fingers, for their gruesome communion" (text in Columbia Records, Masterworks, "The Music of Arnold Schoenberg", I). This song's title invites speculation about the conflicted motivations in Schoenberg's religious identifications, as he was born Jewish, converted to Protestantism, and then returned to the Jewish faith.

Further, anti-Semitic attacks were directed at atonality. For example, one critic suggested that the Jew Schoenberg was inferior and foreign, and thus his music was "purely intellectual, abstract and artificial" – underscoring Wagner's idea that "Jews were incapable of genuine creativity" (Botstein, 1999, p. 39). Since much of the concert-going public in Vienna between 1907 and 1914 was Jewish, Schoenberg's music was thought to constitute a challenge from one Jew to another, particularly regarding the issue of assimilation, to include allegiance or deviance from accepted musical taste.

"Red Mass," with its gruesome text about blood, also evokes speculation about Schoenberg's aggression and his defenses against it that came to be expressed musically, fueling the argument by some musicologists that he deliberately destroyed tonality. Historian Carl Schorske maintains that the composer was launching a criticism against what he perceived to be a "self-deceiving culture" (1981, p. 358). Decrying intellectual complacency and celebrating the "death of the Bourgeois God," Schoenberg composed music that he felt responded to the "inner dictates of mind and instinct" (Schorske, 1981, p. 358).

Whatever psychically fueled Schoenberg's maligned atonal system, in *Pierrot Lunaire* Giraud's poems are compositionally placed in traditional historical forms such as the waltz, passacaglia, and barcarole. It is interesting that the dream and moonlight provided sources of great interest to both Freud and Schoenberg, beginning in 1899 with *The Interpretation of Dreams, Verklarte Nacht, Ewartung,* and *Pierrot Lunaire.* The psychoanalyst was probing manifest and latent material in dreams through verbal and visual representations, and the composer was exploring inner experience through aural and musical techniques.

Pierrot Lunaire aroused vociferous reactions among audiences and music critics worldwide. James Gibbons Huneker wrote the following in the *New York Times* on January 19, 1913:

> I fear and dislike the music of Arnold Schoenberg .... Certainly he is the hardest musical nut to crack of his generation, and the shell is very bitter in the mouth. His moon-stricken Pierrot chants – rather declaims – woes and occasional joys .... It is the DEcomposition [sic] of the art ... enharmonies [sic] that almost made the ears bleed, the eyes water, the scalp to freeze .... There is no melodic or harmonic line, only a series of points, dots, dashes or phrases that sob and scream, despair, explode, exalt, blaspheme ... A man who could portray in tone sheer ugliness with such crystal clearness is to be reckoned with in these topsy-turvy times .... If such music-making is ever to become accepted, then I long for Death the Releaser.
>
> (Cited in Slonimsky, 1953, pp. 153–4)

Musicologist Charles Rosen (1996) notes that dissonance in itself is not a disagreeable sound; rather, "A dissonance is defined by its role in the musical 'language' [similar to the psychoanalytic notion of *contextualization – comment added by JJN*], which makes possible the movement from tension to resolution which is at the heart of what may be generally called expressivity" (p. 25, italics added).

Rosen suggests further that the "emancipation of dissonance" was also an "emancipation of consonance" (p. 26), so that it was no longer necessary to resolve harmonic tensions in diatonic music, which had been fundamental to the "grammar" of harmony and rules of cadences.

The expansion of tonality and the concept of free association are symbolically related under an umbrella of innovations in musical and verbal expression. It is beyond the scope of this discussion to explore: (1) the overdetermined implications of Schoenberg's "destruction" of tonality as a musical commentary about contemporary society in Vienna; (2) his stretching of existing musical expression and technique as a developmental phenomenon in music history; and/ or (3) the composer's intrapsychic torments and defenses against them. Neither do I intend to imply that any musical style is a "simple vehicle for expressing a meaning or emotion" (Rosen, 1996, p. 17), nor that it is the equivalent of any specific psychoanalytic theory or clinical technique. What is clear is that in *fin de siècle* Vienna, both psychoanalyst Freud and composer Schoenberg were exploring internal landscapes as they developed new expressive potentials and new theories about meanings inherent in oral and aural communication.

It was in 1913, one year after the composition of *Pierrot Lunaire,* that Freud made his famous statement about music:

> Works of art do exercise a powerful effect on me, especially those of literature and sculpture, less often painting. This has occasioned me, when I have been contemplating such things, to spend a long time before them, trying to apprehend them in my own way, i.e., to explain to myself what their effect is due to. Wherever I cannot do this, as for instance with music, I am almost incapable of obtaining any pleasure. Some rationalistic, or perhaps analytic, turn of mind in me rebels against being moved by a thing without knowing why I am thus affected, and what it is that affects me.
>
> (1914, *S. E.,* Vol. XIII, p. 211)

Freud's indifference to music is curious since psychoanalytic theory and clinical technique, so dependent on *aural* and *oral* awareness, were developed in the heart of tumultuous, early-twentieth-century Viennese culture. Yet Freud did not pursue music as aural symbolic representation or as a source of psychoanalytic data.

There were some exceptions. In a letter to Fliess in 1897, Freud mentioned his own affective reaction to Wagner's opera *Die Meistersinger:* "I was sympathetically moved by the 'morning dream interpretation melody' ...

Moreover, as in no other opera, real ideas are set to music with the tones of feeling attached to it lingering on as one reflects upon them" (Masson, 1985, p. 286). That Freud was "sympathetically moved" by "tones of feeling" suggests he experienced some affective response to music.

Consider from a psychoanalytic and musical perspective Freud's epistolary comments to his then-fiancée, Martha Bernays:

> I remember something that occurred to me while watching a performance of *Carmen:* the mob gives vent to its appetites, and we deprive ourselves in order to maintain our integrity, we economise in ourselves, our capacity for enjoyment, our relations; and we save ourselves for something, knowing not for what. And this habit of constant suppression of natural instincts gives us the quality of refinement.
>
> (Cited in Cheshire, 1996, p. 1154)

Freud's observation about *Carmen* and his attraction to Wagner's *Die Meistersinger* suggest a possible realization of libidinal containment and restraint that are inherent in music's "rules" (superego representations) that govern meter, imagery, and melody (see Cheshire, 1996). Of further interest is that Freud writes he was "watching" the opera, not "listening" to it or "hearing" the music – implying he was reacting to the mob that appealed to his emphasis on verbal and visual representation.

It is not possible to know whether Freud's reactions were stimulated predominantly by the oral aspects of the libretti, with their oedipal and preoedipal themes and, as mentioned, other features that were visually and verbally representational. Despite his famous disclaimer that "with music, I am almost incapable of obtaining any pleasure" (*S. E.,* Vol. XIII, 1914, p. 211), I suggest that his responses, including his "displeasure" (an affect) were in part stimulated – at least unconsciously – by the structural and formal properties of music, which affectively resonated with his psychoanalytic sensitivities.

From a biographical framework, it has been hypothesized that Freud was disdainful of music because he was jealous of Martha Bernays's relationship with a musician prior to their engagement. We know that, by threatening to leave home, Freud prohibited his musically inclined mother from allowing a piano in the house, thus preventing his younger sister from playing (Abrams, 1993; Barale and Minazzi, 2008). Was his dominance of the household an affective display of jealousy and displaced rivalry (symbolically, with the piano), given that his mother was musical and he did not want to share her attentions and affections either with his father, his sibling, or a musical instrument capable of arousing affect?

Clearly, Freud's reaction to the idea of having a piano in the house was extreme. One biographical hypothesis offers that he rejected music because he was discriminated against as a Jew in anti-Semitic Vienna and tried to distance himself from this environment (Cheshire, 1996). Recall that anti-

Semitism was also ascribed to Schoenberg's music and the composer's reaction to prejudice.

Two musicologists (Adorno, 1952; Sachs, 1945) have puzzled over both Freud's silence about music as it pertains to psychoanalytic theory, and his disclaimers about the effect of music on him. These authors suggest that Wagner's psychoanalytic themes of incest and castration, plus music's capacity to aurally bring the unconscious to consciousness – as dream interpretation can do – were too close for comfort to Freud's own discoveries about dreams.

Others have called Freud's lack of curiosity about music defensive. Some maintain, as he himself did, that he was tone deaf (see Cheshire, 1996). To my ears, there is at least circumstantial evidence that music evoked strong feelings in Freud, which he was unable or unwilling to explore, preferring to "watch" an opera. Although my speculation may be labeled "wild analysis" (Freud, 1910, *S. E.,* Vol. XI, pp. 219–27) by some, I cannot fail to ask what it was that he did not want to hear – or perhaps to feel? Why did Freud come to a halt or take a detour from music as he explored symbolic mental processes that captured his imagination in dreams?

Freud's detour away from music

Barale and Minazzi's (2008) in-depth examination of Freud's attitude toward music suggests that Freud's alternative route to the unconscious and his detour from music was based on more than his rational, biographical disclaimers. In a letter to Fliess dated August 31, 1898, while immersed in composing *The Interpretation of Dreams*, Freud claimed he was stuck at "sound relationships," which "always vexed me because here I lack the most elementary knowledge, thanks to the atrophy of my acoustic sensibilities" (Masson, 1985, p. 324, quoted in Barale and Minazzi, 2008, p. 943).

Yet at the same time that Freud discounted his acoustic sensibilities, he was reading "The Relationships Between Sounds" in *Grundtatsachen* (1883) by Theodore Lipps (1851–1914), a respected German philosopher who had written *Fundamentals of Psychic Life*. Freud was an admirer of Lipps and admitted to Fliess in an 1898 letter that "I found the substance of my insights stated quite clearly in Lipps, perhaps rather more so than I would like" (Masson, 1985, p. 325). Lipps made connections between psychic functioning, empathy, and particularly sound as the underpinning of psychic life. Like other writers at the time, he considered rhythm (particularly the rhythm of psychic experience and its unconscious determinants) to be "ego feeling" or "feeling ego" and empathy (see Martinelli, 2002; Serravezza, 1996, quoted in Barale and Minazzi, 2008).

Pertinent to our discussion about Freud's denial of his acoustic sensibilities is the idea that music, according to Lipps, shifted the focus that Freud was evolving about a representational unconscious in his Dream Books to prerepresentational, nonverbal, affective factors in psychic life. A major divergence between Freud and Lipps regarding music is embedded in Lipps's idea that music was a-semantic, a-rational, and had the "capacity to speak directly to the human mind, to inspire affect in it, and to produce potent unifications prior to and beyond any referential language" (Barale and Minazzi, 2008, p. 944). For Lipps, the aesthetic of music was a central feature of psychic life, irrespective of conscious and unconscious representational factors; in fact, it ultimately gave rise to them.

For Freud, working to develop a scientific theory of mental functioning, such thinking was not consonant, even though it apparently resonated with him. Recall Freud's own account of his inability to obtain pleasure from music: "Some rationalistic, or perhaps analytic, turn of mind in me rebels against being moved by a thing without knowing why I am thus affected and what affects me" (1914a, p. 211).

Yet music was believed to be mystical and a-rational and, as Lipps proposed, it tapped into mental prerepresentations without verbal or visual content. Lipps's theory of psychoanalytic functioning, which included music's capacity to produce powerful affect, could not accommodate Freud's scientific model of the mind, which relied on the pervasive influence of infantile sexuality and on uncovering the repressed to make it accessible to verbal and visual representations.

Interestingly, Freud mentions music in *The Interpretation of Dreams*. His first reference blurs the distinction between auditory and visual imagery as he asserts that dreamers "make use of auditory images as well, and, to a lesser extent, of impressions belonging to the other senses," which he concludes are "residues of verbal presentations" (*S. E.,* Vol. IV, p. 49). Freud maintained that dreamers

> hallucinate – that they replace thoughts by hallucinations. In this respect there is no distinction between visual and acoustic presentations .... If one falls asleep with the memory of a series of musical notes in one's mind, the memory becomes transformed into a hallucination of the same melody ... but during waking, the hallucination gives way to the mnemic presentation.
> (*S. E.,* Vol. IV, p. 50)

While examining modes of representation in dreams, Freud refers to the "mechanism of distortion" (*S. E.,* Vol. V, p. 419n) in describing his analysis of a patient whose neurotic symptoms included "songs or fragments of songs without [the patient's] being able to understand what part they play in her mental life" (*S. E.,* Vol. V, pp. 418–19n). In explaining the dreamer's distortion, Freud makes a distinction between latent and manifest content.

Freud's observations do not advance our understanding of the role of music in mental functioning or of what "fragments of songs" suggest about mental life. Yet it appears that such phrases as "auditory images" and "mechanism of distortion" indicate Freud's awareness, on some level, of the affective, symbolic, and metaphorical qualities of music. For some reason, he did not extend his customarily rigorous curiosity to music and "auditory images," preferring instead to emphasize visual and mnemic representations. That his patient mentioned above was unable – or uninvited by her analyst – to analyze what part songs played in her mental life perhaps sheds more light on the analyst's countertransferential deafness to music than on the patient who dreamed in music.

Thus Freud's theoretical and clinical path embraced language that could verbally represent "something," rather than music as a language of emotions that conveyed an aesthetic and an affect outside the realm of speech, one that perhaps underlay verbal representation. Freud's genius, despite and because of his disclaimers about his tone deafness and lack of acoustical sensibilities, traveled a royal oral road to the unconscious.

Aside from his interest and respect for Lipps's work, Freud was closely connected with noted musicologist/historian Max Graf in Vienna. Psychoanalyst David Abrams (1993) has added significantly to our knowledge regarding Graf's relationship with Freud through his insights into Graf's seminal writings about music and mind.[1] As a close colleague and friend, Graf was a trusted and valued member of Freud's inner circle. In 1902, Graf was invited to join Freud's Wednesday Night Psychoanalytic Society meetings, where he was responsible for "investigating the psychology of great musicians and the process of composing music utilizing psychoanalysis for this task" (Graf, 1942, p. 470). Freud heard Graf's innovative treatises on Beethoven and Wagner during these meetings, although at that point he was more interested in Graf as the father/analyst of "Little Hans" (Max's son, Herbert (Little Hans), subsequently became music director at the Metropolitan Opera in 1936).

Graf's groundbreaking musical studies were based on Freud's early topographic theory, in which Freud maintained that the unconscious could be made conscious through the psychoanalytic method. (Subsequently, Freud revised his topographic theory to the *structural theory,* which allowed for greater complexity in its tripartite model of the mind that involved *id, ego,* and *superego,* rather than his earlier two-dimensional topographic notion of unconscious and conscious levels of mental functioning, which was used by Graf.) Using the conceptual topographic model available to him at the time, Graf maintained that music "functioned for the listener as a way to gain access to the unconscious and as a way to develop increasing psychic balance between the unconscious, preconscious, and conscious levels of the psyche" (Abrams, 1993, p. 301).

Of note, Graf's first publication, with Freud's encouragement, was *Wagner Problems and Other Studies (Wagner Probleme und andere Studien,* 1900), in which he discussed Wagner's personality. Subsequently, Graf published *Richard Wagner and Dramatic Creation (Richard Wagner und das dramatische Schaffen,* 1906), which drew upon the psychoanalytic theory of the time. Here Graf noted that a composer's intrapsychic conflicts paralleled the conflicts of the sociohistorical moment in which he composed. Graf maintained that audience members could relate to the dramatic conflicts portrayed on stage by using the experience to resolve their own intrapsychic conflicts. Later papers by Graf emphasized the sublimation of childhood issues, as well as the idea that artistic expression resulted from both pathological and nonpathological aspects of the personality.

It was in 1910 that Graf published his first book, *The Workshop of a Musician's Mind,* in which he used Freud's 1900 topographical theoretical model of the mind to "analyze" Mozart, Beethoven, and Wagner. The following year, Graf wrote an article called "Richard Wagner in *The Flying Dutchman:* A Contribution to the Psychology of Artistic Creation," which Freud accepted into his own journal, *Writings on Applied Psychology.* This was the first study of a work of music from a psychoanalytic perspective. In it Graf emphasized that a composer creatively represents his own fantasies, conflicts, and inner representational world in sound – particularly when solutions in reality are not available. Graf also emphasized psychoanalytic concepts such as repetition compulsion, identification, early object loss, and maternal fixation (Feder *et al.*, 1990, p. x) in analyzing Wagner's motifs.

Wilheim Stekel, another member of the Wednesday Society, commented that Graf "offered us for the first time a deeper insight into the problem 'Wagner' and had proceeded far beyond what is being offered by extant Wagner biographies" (1911, p. 252). Graf wrote in the foreword that it "would be impossible to separate the ideas which I owe to the guidance of Professor Freud and those which should be attributed to the criticism of several of my colleagues. Thus, I dedicate this study to the memory of those stimulating and exciting hours spent in mutual intellectual striving with this circle of friends" (1911, p. ii).

Abrams (1993) notes that is unclear why Graf discontinued his association with the Wednesday Society in 1912. Subsequently, Graf spent many years in New York City, where he continued to write about Vienna (*Legend of a Musical City*, 1945; *Modern Music*, 1946; and *Composer and Critic*, 1946). Returning to Vienna in 1947, Graf reworked his 1910 book *From Beethoven to Shostakovich: The Psychology of the Composing Process.* His last book (*Every Hour Was Filled,* 1957), written years after his membership in the Wednesday Society in the early years of the century, contained his reminiscences of Freud. In describing his numerous consultations with Freud, Graf noted that "Freud welcomed conversations with a musician which gave him access to a field unfamiliar to him, and our initial acquaintance developed into friendship" (1957, p. 163). Graf died in 1958 at the age of eighty-four.

One can recognize certain tributes to Freud in Graf's work as probable transferences, marking a similarity with the way that Graf also idealized and experienced the role of a music conductor as someone who "came, sat at his desk, opened the sorcerer's book and raised his magic wand" (1945, pp. 67–8). The synergy between the two men can be imagined even in the absence of a fuller explanation. Clearly, Max Graf was as much a pioneer for his recognition of the convergence between psychoanalysis and music as he was in regard to the well-known analysis of his son Herbert, "Little Hans" (Freud, 1909a). Given his heritage, it is not hard to understand why Herbert Graf gravitated professionally to the field of opera, an art form combining words and music; he became a producer of opera – including, as mentioned, a director of the Metropolitan Opera in New York City.

Freud wrote a great deal about affects, including shame, humiliation, envy, and greed. His Dream Books set forth his theories about displacement, multiple determinism, metaphor/symbolism, latent and manifest content, and primary and secondary processes. He applied these concepts clinically to the nonverbal, visual, and oral representational realms of mental life. Yet he did not develop a formal theory of affect about "the direct language of live emotions, temporality, and the underlying tuning of psychic life" (Barale and Minazzi, 2008, p. 947). Freud's interests remained academic, while music, comprised of symbolic, highly organized nonverbal sounds, was thought to be "a-semantic" (see Barale, 1997).

Conceptualized in this manner, music as it pertains to affect and meaning is beyond the scope and understanding of science. Clearly, to Freud, music was a-scientific, and so there remained a divergence between music and mind on Freud's oral road to the unconscious.

The aural/oral road converges

Despite Freud's disclaimers about music and without his benediction, the auditory sphere has long provided fascination to others interested in the aesthetics of reception, affect, sound, and nonverbal representation in psychic life. In the discipline of philosophy, in 1823, Hegel referred to music as "the symbolic and expressive equivalent of the time of interiority itself" (quoted in Barale and Minazzi, 2008, p. 940). In psychoanalysis, Abraham (1914) included auditory factors regarding the *Sexualtheorie,* while Isakower (1939) published "On the Exceptional Position of the Auditory Sphere." Theodor Reik compared the analytic attitude with musical listening and labeled the analyst's unconscious a "musical instrument" (quoted in Barale and Minazzi, 2008, p. 938). Susanne Langer, also a philosopher, conceptualized music as sound without content that was connected to the "very movement of psychic life in its … preverbal structure" (quoted in Barale and Minazzi, 2008, p. 939).

Heinz Kohut (1957), an innovative psychoanalytic thinker, maintained that music was related to secondary (rational, problem-solving) processes, serving the mature ego in a psychic hierarchy in which it was preceded by primary (primitive and preverbal) processes. This stance maintained that primary and secondary processes were discreet, and that secondary process developmentally superseded a-rational, primary-process mental activity. Ernst Kris's seminal 1952 studies on creativity concluded that nonpathological regression to primitive primary process occurred "in service of the ego" (p. 177). His conceptualization, implying a nonpathological but inflexible, bi-phasic, hierarchical model, prevailed for many years, maintaining that the ego and higher-level secondary processes structured the chaos of subordinate primary process mental activity.

Contemporary psychoanalytic commentary by Noy (2009) and Wilson (2009), and empirical research by Brakel (2002, 2007) – as well as the concepts of symmetry and asymmetry, as set forth by Matte Blanco (1981) and revisited by Lombardi (2009), pertaining to the mental metabolization of music in listeners – suggests that primary process is not exclusively, or even necessarily, connected with conflict, regression, or psychopathology. Further, primary and secondary processes, the fantasy/unstructured and reality/concrete dichotomies of mental life, are not discrete and hierarchical, but rather exist in oscillation; they are dynamic, and both simultaneously contribute to the regulation of contrasting emotions. Thus, not only is music capable of arousing emotion (Noy, 1993, 2009; Langer, 1942; Feder, 1993, 2004; Nagel, 2007, 2008a, 2008b, 2010), it is also believed that *multiple* acoustic stimuli are fluidly, continually, and simultaneously – or polyphonically – represented and processed in the mind.

Conceptualizations about primary and secondary processes, elucidated in Freud's *The Interpretation of Dreams*, are relevant to the psychoanalytic theories of development as well as to psychoanalytic treatment. Particularly pertinent are the ideas that preoedipal and oedipal dynamics are fluid, and that dyadic and triadic dynamics and relationships are not hierarchical, "either/or" phenomena – that is, *either* intrapsychic *or* relational.

Clinical vignette

Thoughts about the fluidity and timelessness of mental life remind me of an elderly patient I saw, who at an advanced age was vigorous and successful professionally. She wanted to work through some unfinished business from early childhood regarding her experience of parental neglect. Events from many years ago were affecting her current relationships, as well as her self-esteem. Her relationship with me and with her family members shed light on the ultimate terror of a young child: that of being left and unloved.

As my patient's intellectual understanding of her emotional memories became affectively palpable in the transference, she commented, "I never thought I'd be working on these kinds of issues at my age." In reaching an understanding of her upsetting and persistent depressive and anxious symptoms that originally brought her to treatment, we traversed back and forth between our relationship, her current and past relationships, traumas involving illnesses in her family of origin, and the almost intolerable affects around aloneness that continued to haunt her.

Over time, we connected the dots to her earliest, partially remembered – but currently re-experienced – screen memories, which triggered affects about loss and attendant affects of overwhelming anxiety. We continually found ourselves weaving back and forth on a road between primary and secondary processes, affects and bodily sensations, preoedipal traumas regarding loss and being left alone, current worries about being forgotten and left out, her own mortality and her defenses against it, illnesses of family members, parenting and aging, loss of her contemporaries through death, and oedipal-like competitive conflicts in her ongoing creative work.

Although overt references to music were not a part of our work together, this patient's clinical picture poignantly illustrates the fluidity and persistence of consonant and dissonant mental melodies and their derivatives. Such melodies of the mind and their vicissitudes ebb and flow with fluidity throughout the physical and psychological lifespan. In this instance, the therapeutic journey on an oral road provided the patient with a way to consolidate, understand, and integrate her memories and their powerful influence, resulting in considerable relief.

Ehrenzweig (1953) posited that music originates unconsciously in its creator, and, similarly to what happens in a dream, it is "deciphered and comprehended" by the "language of the unconscious" (quote cited in Noy, 1993, p. 130). Ehrenzweig doubted that it was ever to "be hoped ... to translate the symbolic message of music in rationally comprehensible words" (1953, p. 64).

Some years later, this same author commented that:

> It is not unreasonable to speculate that speech and music have descended from a common origin in a primitive language . . . . Later this primeval language would have split into different branches: music would have retained the articulation mainly by pitch (scale) and duration (rhythm), while language chose the articulation mainly by tone colour (vowels and consonants) . . . . Music has become a symbolic language of the unconscious mind.
>
> (Ehrenzweig, 1975, pp. 164–5)

Ehrenzweig implies that words are necessary to communicate on a secondary-process level about nonverbal, primary-process aspects of music, but – and perhaps most important – his observations also lead to the more inclusive suggestion that both oral *and* aural roads form connecting pathways to mental life, rendering an either/or explanation reductionistic.

Friedman (1960) offers: "A musical theme represents an affect which temporarily activates some unconscious conflict" (p. 448). Noy (1967b) describes musical structure as "analogous to the dream, daydream, or joke ... and [it] can be analyzed by psychoanalytic techniques to reveal its latent content" (p. 45). Feder's (1993a) work on music and mind examine music itself as a point of entry into mental processes, as he explores the importance of the tonality of D minor in Mozart's *Don Giovanni* – an opera Freud enjoyed – noting that this tonality connoted themes of fathers and fathering.

Feder also analyzed the harmonic modulation from A flat major to E major in Schubert's "Moment Musicale," Opus 94, No. 6, from a musical and affective framework. In this context, he emphasized a single note, "a promissory E-natural," framed by provisos pertaining to exaggerated claims regarding both clinical and applied methodology, serving both as a "pivotal nodal point … and a mental organizer and integrator" of psychic life (1993b, p. 14). Avoiding reductionism and tidy explanations, Feder underscores the psychic functions of music and connections between affect and idea, feeling and meaning.

As we think developmentally about parent–child interactions and auditory sensitivity, Winnicott's concept of "transitional phenomena" can be applied to the aural sphere and transitional tunes (McDonald, 1970), raising questions about early parent–child relationships cradled in meaningful nonverbal sounds. Kohut and Levarie (1950) addressed the psychological correlates of melody, tonality, rhythm, and repetition as they examined the elements and function of musical form, suggesting that sounds come from both external stimuli and internal sources that have – or develop – affective significance through associations. For the infant, sound can be threatening or soothing, creating tension and/or relief. Mother's voice ideally becomes associated with gratification, tension reduction, and pleasure, while silence (and/or certain noises) may be threatening and anxiety producing, and may evoke, by extension, abandonment and aloneness.

Conversely, mother and father can be responsive to or ignore their child's earliest nonverbal gurgles, coos, and cries, thereby establishing a foundation for psychic attunement to intimacy and safety on the one hand, or anxiety and danger on the other. Following a long pause in her session, one of my patients recounted, "I get anxious when it is silent here … a song in my head eases anxiety." Analysis revealed that her anxiety was related to her embarrassment and fear of abandonment by me should she speak freely. This belief was related to the impending termination of her analysis, as well as to earlier historical determinants of parental emotional insensitivity, experienced by the patient as rejection. She also spoke of vague memories about comforting lullabies that had been hummed to her in childhood by her grandmother during a life-threatening illness, providing a sense of safety that existed side by side with empathetic failures in parent–child exchanges.

Unlike silence, mother's or father's voice – and, by extension, fantasies about the analyst's voice – can be loud and frightening. Such was also the case for this patient, who feared her father's explosive temper and his thunderous voice, highlighting the multiply determined meanings inherent in sounds as well as words. Rose (1993, 2004) draws on developmental issues, psychoanalytic concepts, and neuroscientific data to explicate connections between "perceptual stimuli … and affective meanings"; he believes that "music provides the perceptual preconditions for affect" (1993, p. 79).

While beyond the scope of this discussion yet clearly relevant, it should be noted that both observations of nonverbal communications in infant–parent interactions and neurophysiology research are pertinent and can deepen our understanding of the function of music and sounds in mental life. Suffice it to emphasize here that, from the earliest moments of life, there is a "pool of music and sound in which a baby is bathed" (Imberty, 2002b, quoted in Barale and Minazzi, 2008, p. 948). A "sound envelope" (Anzieu, 1976) evolves into language and affects that define relational exchanges with others. A concert of early aural experiences and nonverbal interactions precedes and defines object constancy, object loss, social interactions, and self-definition.

Despite divergences – both conceptual and expressive ones – music and psychoanalytic theory convey a language, with one expressed aurally while the other is articulated verbally. Both modes of communication adhere to a particular canon, a specific set of rules governing style, grammar, and form. Both are replete with metaphors, with symbols and symbolic meanings representing the literal, obvious, and manifest as well as the abstract, concealed, and latent. Both adhere to theory. Both transcend any single theory.

Given these complex characteristics and parameters, how might one attempt to bridge music and mind, or mind and music? As emphasized by Feder (1993b), "wild psychoanalysis" and "wild musicology" – the application of musical and psychological interpretive meaning without a critical examination of underlying formal assumptions, theories, and methodology – justifies objections. Yet both inside and outside the consulting room and the concert hall, it is possible to present good enough evidence to bridge this divergence. Foremost is the necessity to avoid reductionistic, formulaic, oppositional, "either/or" dichotomies. Embracing an attitude of "also/and" enriches our thinking while simultaneously acknowledging limitations and avoiding exaggerated claims about either music or psychoanalysis. The bridge that spans music, affect, and mental processes is built upon thoughtful, good enough evidence about how one arrives at conclusions, interpretations, and complex understandings.

Bridging the gap

Using music itself as psychoanalytic data, Feder (1993b) proposed that stylistic features of a musical composition may shed light on mental processes and the structure of the mind in general. In order to highlight concepts shared by music and psychoanalysis – i.e., *feeling* and *meaning, affect* and *idea* – Feder *et al.* examined three principles, well-known in clinical psychoanalysis and emphasized in *The Interpretation of Dreams*, as theoretical entries for bridging the conceptual gap between mind and music and making the "mysterious leap" from mind to art (1993b, p. 10). These include (1) overdeterminism and multiple function; (2) infinite displaceability; and (3) infinite representation.

Overdeterminism, a fundamental concept generated by Freud (1900), considers all interpretations of mental life to be embedded in a broad context.

In other words, a thought, feeling, idea, and/or a creation of music or art is stimulated by multiple factors contributing to multidimensional layers of depth and breadth of meaning. Roy Schafer (1983) speaks to the psychoanalytic concepts of overdeterminism and multiple function when he notes that psychoanalysts do not talk about "what something really means." Rather, Schafer notes:

> That one has discovered further meaning, weightier meaning, more disturbing meaning, more archaic meaning, or more carefully disguised meaning than that which first met the eye or ear does not justify the claim that one has discovered the ultimate truth that lies behind the world of appearances – the "real" world.
>
> (1983, p. 8)

Compositional choices and affective reactions to them are also multidetermined elements in psychic life. The fluidity of mental processes enables one idea, thought, sound, or feeling to represent another. Emphasized here is the notion that multiply determined mental representations are infinitely displaceable. As observed by Feder (1993b), that which is visual and symbolic can be represented in the auditory sphere, a view that Freud could not or would not explore in relation to music. When we adopt the view that music and mental life symbolically share multiple meanings and displaceability, we can entertain the idea that symbols of music and mental life are infinitely represented in a variety of oral and aural themes and variations.

Psychodynamic concepts of overdeterminism, displacement, and multiple function are illustrated in Feder's (1990a,b; 1992) studies of American composer Charles Ives. The auditory sphere and the connection between the composer's relationship with his father, his creative output, and the "fantasy of the 'ear'" (Feder, 1990a, p. 154) are emphasized. Ives's ear was viewed as the "organ of creativity" (Feder, 1990a, p. 154), which metaphorically displaced and extended its auditory function.

In his own book, *Memos* (1972), Ives recalls being told by his father, "If you must play a chromatic scale, play it like a man" (cited in Feder, 1990a, p. 155), and continued, "Music has always been an emasculated art" (cited in Feder, 1990a, p. 156). Feder noted a recurrent theme of "disuse atrophy" (p. 156), citing Ives's own words: "There may be an analogy between (or at least similar process) of the ear, the mind, and arm muscles. They don't get strong with disuse" (Ives, 1972, p. 42; cited in Feder, 1990a, p. 156).

Implied in this statement is a fear of castration or injury, i.e., disuse embedded in the displacement upward from the genitals to the ear, Ives's primary organ, which he valued both for hearing and creating, receiving and producing. Relevant to our discussion here, the meaning of the Ivesian ear points to the psychoanalytic concept of *multiple function,* since the ear is conceptualized as a pathway to the mind and meaning. Certainly, Ives conceived and produced ear-stretching music in his blending of familiar and new melodies, folk songs, textures, harmonies, and tone clusters.

Like Ives, each of us develops and affectively adheres to a variety of mental displacements and compromises that represent our earliest meaningful relationships and body functions. In this example, music has the capability, through the auditory realm, to serve as a catalyst to illustrate complex mental processes – a function more commonly attributed to visual and oral verbal representations. The psychoanalyst knows that mental representations can be displaced, just as the musician knows that harmonies can modulate, be transposed, or manipulated tonally, atonally, and serially. In the following chapters, I will explore themes emphasizing that the *aural* sphere is viable, along with the *visual* and the *verbal*, as a pathway to affect and symbolic representation in mental life.

Before proceeding to the case-ette chapters, where particular music compositions will be offered as quasi-clinical psychoanalytic data, I will present a clinical vignette highlighting the intersection between the music of speech and the language of music in the consulting room.

Clinical vignette

Ms. T was a violinist who consulted me for help with her performance anxiety. At our initial sessions, she expressed worry about her technical security when "playing fast passages." She said that her technique fell apart when she was anxious, and that this had increasingly become a problem for her. Although she wanted to be a soloist, she had become involved in chamber music while in school and currently played second violin in a string quartet.

Ms. T had never previously experienced physical discomfort while playing the violin, but during the period of treatment under discussion, she developed pain in her bow arm, for which she consulted numerous physicians. Although no underlying physiological condition was diagnosed, she was neither satisfied with nor cured by purely physiological approaches. The phrase coined in Bobby McFerrin's song, "Don't Worry, Be Happy," was not curative for Ms. T, as medical findings to the contrary and physician reassurance did not diminish her symptoms. In fact, she continued to search for the "right answer" – a theme that emerged early in her work with me.

The nature of Ms. T's resistance to medical and psychological treatment was related to childhood trauma and repressed affects that resulted, in part, in the displacement of her pain from the psychological to the physical. Of note is that her pain escalated and coincided with her growing professional success. As her career blossomed, so did other issues, including pain.

Ms. T was approaching graduation from a prestigious conservatory when she came to me with severe stage fright. She decided to try psychotherapy following a disastrous performance. She told me that her stage fright had been lifelong and had been unresponsive to self-help measures. Her symptoms were not unusual – i.e., shaking, and a fear that her lack of technical capability would be exposed in public.

Ms. T had pursued a music career to her parents' disapproval; furthermore, they had brought her up to believe that "smart people can solve their own problems, and only crazy people go to therapists." Thus her seeking mental health treatment was a defiant act, as well as an admission of being "dumb and crazy." It was not surprising to discover her ambivalence about treatment with me as it emerged in our work. Her most striking characteristic was that she wanted immediate "answers" from me, just as she demanded all the right notes from herself in a performance.

My attempts to help Ms. T explore her thoughts and to view things from a different perspective were perceived as criticisms. Often, sessions felt like battles during which she tried to coerce me into working with her in the way she thought a therapist should work. Frequently, she found flaws in my comments. Treatment became a competition, and her argumentativeness was at odds with her simultaneous wish to keep the peace at all costs. Her tactics frequently left me feeling blocked and impotent as a clinician, as my attempts to collaborate were relentlessly rebuffed. Often I would feel as helpless as she no doubt felt, which led me to realize that what I experienced in my countertransference was the temptation to treat her as she treated me – i.e., to argue.

Ms. T frequently referred to her childhood fear of her father's temper, to which she would respond by "kicking and screaming" – the same reaction she was reliving with me in her verbal attacks. Her mother's inability to meet her need for security had compounded her narcissistic injuries. Now, her anxiety about displeasing her quartet colleagues and her audiences, thus losing their respect and love, was an extension of the theme of power and submission that was shaping her interactions in treatment as well as on stage.

In short, this competent, bright, and talented woman was presenting herself as an overwhelmed, helpless victim. Her insistence on answers from me replayed a time in her life when she was a dependent child and the target of parental bullying and emotional abuse and neglect. Thus, our interaction recapitulated a pattern in which she felt victimized, yet she continually abdicated control at the same time she demanded it. It gradually became clear that her survival depended on perfect performances – not only her own, but those of the people from whom she wanted nurturance as well.

Despite her unrelenting complaints about feeling no better, Ms. T remained in treatment, and by the second year of our work together, her quartet had begun to receive considerable acclaim. Following a concert at the end of her third year in therapy, she complained that she had developed a pain in her bow arm. Her mounting musical success led to intense practicing, which took precedence over everything else, including her relationship with her fiancé. Convinced that I could not really help her, she began a pilgrimage to many physicians for relief of her arm pain. Numerous tests and consultations confirmed no organic damage. Rest, physical therapy, and ice were recommended. Only one physician suggested that she pay attention to emotional issues, while another discounted psychological distress altogether and recommended evaluation for exploratory surgery.

Since Ms. T could not obtain "answers" from me or from her physicians, she complained more vehemently about the deficiencies of our work. Yet she did not find relief from pain in a regimen that now included physical therapy, massage, and stress reduction classes. A growing concern about losing the ability to play altogether and needing to change careers began to escalate. I continued to question her reluctance to examine her emotional life to find the source of her pain; it seemed to me that physical pain and sadomasochistic enactments were her signature style.

Following an argument with her fiancé, Ms. T related to me with surprise that he had been very nice to her the next day. She described his behavior as "disarming" and said, "Since I didn't want to rock the boat, I didn't really show him my anger." Clearly, for Ms. T, expressing strong feelings or raising her voice (or her arm) was dangerous, leading to the risk of separation and loss.

This session was followed by a dream in which Ms. T feared losing the affection of a famous man with whom she was romantically involved. When he had to travel on a business trip, she feared he would never return. Although she was excited and happy to see him when he came back, she could not show it, and was able only to whisper to him, "I love you."

A turning point in our work came when Ms. T suddenly announced her decision to discontinue therapy with me. While she appeared assertive in her stance, she was also obviously upset, viscerally so, as she spoke. She said she felt I wasn't helping her and added, "I expect you to make things easier for me."

I responded to her distressed affect by asking if she could find words for her feelings. Surprisingly, she responded that it felt as though she were having a childish temper tantrum – "I want to hit and hurt someone." I wondered aloud whether she might want to hurt me. She began to cry and spoke of a "tug of war" between us. I replied that I thought the tug of war was inside her, although she considered me to be her enemy.

Another session passed without Ms. T expressing any further plan to leave the treatment. She did note that she had been tempted to break up with her fiancé. She said, "I think I drive people crazy and they won't want to be around me." I suggested that perhaps she thought she would drive me crazy with her noxious thoughts, and that I would become disgusted and send her away. She commented that she would like to be more "spontaneous and not so constipated, but treatment seems endless. I think you'll surprise me one day and say we're done."

I pointed out that this was exactly what she herself had done with her sudden announcement about quitting; perhaps she needed to leave me in order to avoid being abandoned and rejected by someone whom she cared about. Ms. T admitted, "I threw a tantrum." I noted that she had said she felt like hurting me. She replied, "I guess I did so verbally."

At her next session, Ms. T spoke at length of how she had been too busy with concerts and stress reduction classes to think about relationship issues. I observed that she was choosing to focus on her activities rather than on herself and her thoughts and feelings. She began to argue that I was criticizing her, and it felt like "being slapped in the face." Recalling her descriptions of her father and his temper, I asked, "Did your father ever slap you in the face?"

Ms. T replied, "I was always afraid. Most of all, I fear anger from others . . . . I fear they will either hit me or hate me." I interpreted her projection and said, "I think you also fear your own anger – that you will be the one to hit or lash out or somehow hurt me. You keep it inside because it is so psychologically painful, but at the same time your arm is so painful that it can't function. I think the pain that disables your arm actually protects you from feeling that at any moment you may hit me."

Following a very lengthy pause, Ms. T spoke of a recent concert, "The pain in my arm went away when I played, and also the day afterward. I felt like I could play anything! I have a number of performances coming up, but I'm still worrying I won't be able to play." I responded, "It sounds as though something frightens you about being too good – and also about being free of pain."

Ms. T's wish to leave me was not surprising. She was remembering in the transference and re-enacting a relationship from her past as she externalized blame onto me, on "the music profession," and on her "insensitive fiancé." She cast herself in the role of a helpless and submissive victim as she re-created a sadomasochistic relationship between parent and child that revolved around issues of power and submission. Her feeling of pressure to perform well in treatment as well as on stage was defended against both by her sense of helplessness and her demanding attitude as she placed me in the role of the betraying authority figure who had the expertise to ease her pain, but selfishly and cruelly withheld relief.

It became clear that Ms. T's attitude enabled her to identify with her abusive and demeaning father. This role and gender reversal provided her with the omnipotence she craved, feeling she lacked any power. In this way she could be both the punitive adult and the defiant child. Since she experienced my interpretations as assaults that she vigorously repelled, I found myself either withholding my comments in order to avoid confrontations, or becoming more verbal than is usually comfortable for me. As I became aware of how manipulative she was and of my own increasing irritation and impatience, it was clearer to me that her statement about withdrawing from treatment was a way of protecting herself from what she feared would turn into mutually expressed rage and destruction of both of us. She wanted to strike out at me and leave me before I could strike her or, worse, abandon her.

It was not surprising, therefore, to find Ms. T consulting many medical specialists; she was desperate to seek out "answers" as she simultaneously provided herself with a network of back-up caretakers should her relationship with me collapse. Her unrelenting search for solutions from authority figures reflected the depth of her longing for love and protection from her earliest caregivers. She wanted reassurance from me and the other doctors that she was okay – not damaged physically or defective emotionally. Her strategies fueled her illusion of omnipotence and camouflaged her underlying aching feeling of helplessness, her panic about separation, and her fears of terrifying loss. Her characteristic style was reflected in her conflicted attachment to her piercing physical pain, which sometimes surfaced, displaced, in the guise of performance anxiety symptoms.

Ms. T's emotional pain was multiply determined and displaced from the psychic to the physical sphere and held overdetermined meanings for her. In the consulting room, I paid close attention to her affects, metaphors and fantasies, her dreams regarding abandonment by those on whom she depended, her tendency to enact with me the very abandonments she feared, and the displacement of other multiply determined dynamics in transference and other relationships – all lurking latently beneath her manifest presenting complaint of performance anxiety based on insecurity about her technical skill and memory while on stage. In working with her, I was aware of the fluidity of action and mentation as I experienced her core dynamics as multiply determined leitmotivs that revealed her contrapuntal psychic melodies.

Intrapsychic and interpersonal issues that are represented preverbally and nonverbally are unconsciously preserved, ever ready to be awakened and reawakened by internal and external stimuli – through words and/or music or other stimuli. Yet, the psychoanalytic literature is far from saturated with articles about music's effect on patients. There is much to gain in the consulting room by tuning in to the patient's musical associations and experiences and the analyst's reactions to them. Sonic signifiers inherent in music have the capacity to evoke latent fantasies, screen memories, and bodily sensations which in turn can link the psychic past with the present, affect with idea, feeling (including preverbal and prerepresentational) with meaning. Aren't these part of the goals of our clinical work?

Music as psychoanalytic data

Notably absent in the psychoanalytic literature is the analysis of *music itself* from psychoanalytic perspectives. This is not unusual, as one would not expect all psychoanalysts to be proficient in music, any more than one would expect all musicians to be well versed in psychoanalysis. However, the lack of theory and method regarding an intersection between psychoanalysis and music need not inhibit such an exploration. Added to our repertoire, its inclusion can increase our awareness of possible uses of music and psychoanalytic theory to explicate nonverbal processes and interpersonal communications. This endeavor holds the potential to deepen our understanding of the interweaving, of the divergences and convergences between music and psychoanalysis. With these multidetermined challenges in mind, and drawing upon my own hybrid background, I will use music itself as psychoanalytic data in the following chapters. In doing so, mindful of my biases, I do not attempt to empirically prove or disprove my ideas about music as psychoanalytic data, or to equate applied psychoanalysis with actual clinical processes reliant on the use of transference, countertransference, and resistance interpretations.

In his book *Retelling a Life* (1992), Schafer addresses issues pertinent to our discussion regarding "interdisciplinary conversations" (p. 165) between clinical psychoanalysts and critical theorists. Addressing the question of how do we "know," Schafer not only probes how one arrives at a "sense of an answer" (p. 166 – a phrase he uses to explore the concept of psychoanalytic evidence and also the title of his particular chapter), he discusses the intersections and divergences between clinical and applied psychoanalysis. To illustrate, Schafer uses the theme and variations of the fairy tale of Snow White and two clinical vignettes to show how multiple theoretical constructs can "explain" underlying dynamics, from both applied and clinical perspectives. In doing so, Schafer demonstrates how Freudian theory, object relations theory, and self psychology can all elucidate the complexity of multiply determined mental processes. Important questions are raised for psychoanalysts. How does one establish "evidence"; how does one "know" through the use of clinical theory and technique and/or through applied interpretation?

By drawing attention to the oft-heard claim that in applied psychoanalysis there is "no patient to talk back" (p. 174), Schafer underscores how the clinical encounter is but one form of psychoanalytic understanding, maintaining that "first person speech is inherently problematic" (p. 174) when interpreting the speaker's story. Applying psychoanalytic concepts outside the clinical situation is believed to be equally valid in the quest for a "sense of an answer," yet an applied approach is relegated, by some, to a lower status than clinical practice in the psychoanalytic hierarchy. Schafer calls for considering the specific issues inherent in both clinical and applied/interdisciplinary work, where the "specific content [is] being defined within the specific context being established" (p. 175). Thus, the psychoanalyst becomes the co-author of oral as well as written and aural "texts," searching for answers, and "clinical and applied analysis emerge as versions of one psychoanalysis, with no clear-cut parasitic relationship of one to the other. Both amount to the same work carried out under varied conditions" (p. 186). As Schafer notes, perhaps the attainment of the "sense of an answer" leads to a "changed sense of the questions" (p. 186) in attempts to unearth meaning.

I agree with Feder *et al.* (1993) and Noy (2009) that the multiple and formal qualities of music, e.g., harmony, rhythm, melody, dynamics, tonal centers, etc., and their creative displacements and compositional manipulations by the composer, allow the listener to better integrate and achieve multiple levels of complex mental polyphony. Our appreciation of this musicological underpinning, explicated in the case-ette chapters in which music itself is conceptualized as quasi-clinical data, can lead to thoughtful assumptions and discussion about music and mental processes.

Although I will hold to the spirit of analyzing particular music examples "as if" they are psychoanalytic data, I do not imply that either music or psychoanalytic concepts, with their exquisite capacities for multiple function, infinite representation, displaceability, fluidity, and nonverbal essence, is reducible to any singular theory of mind or theoretical perspective. Convincing arguments can be made for a relationship between music and psychoanalytic concepts based upon other psychoanalytic, philosophical, and musicological frameworks. In other forums, music from cultures other than the Western classical tradition that I have chosen can and should be analyzed.

While noting and emphasizing Freud's supposed aversion or ambivalence toward music, I leave it to others to speculate further about why he avoided recognizing its relevance in mental life. In throwing into high relief the chasm between scientific and aesthetic, aural and oral, and representational and prerepresentational, it is my intention to propose that these polarities can be bridged, and thereby contribute to a past, present, and future interdisciplinary dialogue with which to consider innovative pathways to conceptualize music and mental life.

We can use our curiosity about affects and their latent meanings as they may be related to drives and their derivatives, to object relationships, and to the multiple functions of the ego expressed through extraordinary nonverbal – or *musical* – pathways to develop creative ways to think about psychoanalytic and musical theory, applied psychoanalysis, and clinical practice. That music is a point of entry into affect, meaning, pre-verbal representations, and unconscious processes is compatible with Feder's (2004) proposal that music is a simulacrum of mental life, as well as Noy's (2009) statement that music reflects a "'sum-total' of all disparate and opposing emotions," leading to what he calls a "meta-emotion" (p. 1).

It is time – indeed, past time – to use an interdisciplinary roadmap to explore how musical and psychoanalytic concepts intersect and inform each other, how music *itself* is pertinent psychoanalytic data, how music is a point of entry into affect, how music and mental processes converge on oral/aural roads, and how music and psychoanalytic ideas have relevance and significance both inside and outside the consulting room and the concert hall. Conceptualized both as symbolic representations and prerepresentations of emotional life in sound, musical elements and psychoanalytic principles are tandem vehicles on this fascinating excursion. The case-ettes that follow, based upon specific musical examples, are invitations to travel a road less taken.

Part II

Moods and melodies

Chapter 2

Case-ette 1

Ambiguity – The Tritone in "Gee, Officer, Krupke" (West Side Story)

We never got the love that ev'ry child ought-a get!
(Jets singing to Office Krupke, vocal score, p. 173)

There's a time for us, someday a time for us .... We'll find a new way of living .... We'll find a way of forgiving .... Somehow, someday, somewhere!
(A Girl, vocal score, pp. 163–5)

The out-of-town advance reviews for *West Side Story* raved in August 1957. The *Washington Post* called the new musical "a uniquely cohesive comment on life .... The violence is senseless but Leonard Bernstein's score makes us feel what we do not understand." The *Daily News* said the show opened "a new field in the American stage" (quoted in Burton, 1994, p. 271).

West Side Story opened in New York City on September 26, 1957. Drama critic Walter Kerr wrote in the *Herald Tribune,* "The radioactive fallout from *West Side Story* must still be descending on Broadway this morning," while Brooks Atkinson of the *Times* called the show "profoundly moving ... as ugly as the city jungles and also pathetic, tender and forgiving .... The subject is not beautiful, but what *West Side Story* draws out of it is beautiful. For it has a searching point of view" (Kerr and Atkinson quoted in Burton, 1994, p. 276).

The award-winning, always poignant *West Side Story,* which enjoyed an updated Broadway revival in the spring of 2009, cross-pollinates music and theater, as well as music and psychoanalytic concepts.[1] While the critical reviews of *West Side Story* just cited are unambiguous, its story and music are replete with subtle and contradictory messages and meanings. Manifestly an update of *Romeo and Juliet,* with the themes of forbidden love and rivalries acted out between clashing gangs and cultures – i.e., the Caucasian Jets and the Puerto Rican Sharks – the story of this musical encompasses so much more.

Composer Leonard Bernstein's unquenchable thirst for knowledge and boundless curiosity about how internal and external events intersect are pertinent to our discussion regarding musical and psychoanalytic ambiguity seen throughout the score of *West Side Story,* and specifically in the song "Gee, Officer Krupke." Bernstein creates a bridge between the concert stage and the Broadway orchestra pit through his musical treatment of ambiguity, which invites reflection about intrapsychic processes, interpersonal relationships, sociocultural norms, and the uses of psychoanalytic thinking in relation to community, social, and global problems, as well as the significance of the aural sphere in mental life.

While these contrapuntal themes will be interwoven throughout this chapter, my focus is centered upon the importance and use of the musical interval called the *tritone* (which will be explained in what follows) in *West Side Story*. I conceptualize Bernstein's use of the tritone as *sonic psychoanalytic data;* i.e., the use of the *music itself* is evidence that is metaphorically akin to the clinical processes of free association, transference, countertransference, resistance, and other psychoanalytic concepts.

As noted in the preceding chapter, there has been an ongoing skepticism about the methodology of applied psychoanalytic studies and "good enough" evidence expressed by psychoanalysts of various theoretical orientations. It is not my intention to make "truth" claims. Rather, my aim is to present psychoanalytically informed *inferences* versus *interpretations* through an exploration of the use of the tritone in *West Side Story* (and in other music in my subsequent case-ettes). These musical examples all accord with my belief that there is a connection between musical and psychoanalytic concepts that is integral to affect and unconscious processes. Therefore, sonic psychoanalytic data contribute to a musical-psychoanalytic appreciation of the subtleties of musical and mental ambiguity. In this case, the tritone as used throughout *West Side Story* and especially in "Gee, Officer Krupke" represents a sonic metaphor for ambiguity, restlessness, and instability. As we listen, we are drawn into a search for tonal and emotional resolution that reflects the young characters' profound inner turmoil.

Music arouses and conveys emotion in and to listeners (Noy, 1993, 2009; Langer, 1942; Feder *et al.*, 1990, 1993, Feeder, 2004; Nagel, 2007, 2008a,b, 2010a,b), and the listener mentally processes music in a manner that organizes acoustic stimuli. Specifically, Feder (1993b) proposed that music evokes feeling and meaning, affect and idea, and Noy (2009) claimed that music not only evokes emotion in listeners, but also reflects a "'sum-total' of all the disparate and opposing emotions" (p. 1). These phenomena find an analogy in the power of film to move us emotionally in a way that we must also inwardly process. Gabbard (1997) noted that the audience-spectator creates meaning from what is visually generated on the screen.

The tritone – with its musical heritage of being considered an abrasive interval, originally associated with the devil – provides a unique opportunity for us to examine conflicts and affects in mental life as expressed by its use in a musical score.

Ambiguity and the tritone: *diabolus in musica*

For centuries, composers and music theorists have been aware of the instability and ambiguity of the musical interval (i.e., the space between one musical note and the next) called the *tritone* (Drabkin, 2001, in Groves, pp. 747–9). As we begin to orient ourselves to the tritone, we should keep in mind that the intervals of the twelve-tone (or *chromatic*) scale – the tuning of equal temperament in Western culture – are all half steps. In the eight-note, major and minor, octave scales of the Western diatonic musical tradition, the intervals between notes follow patterns of both whole and half steps.

The tritone interval is comprised of three whole tones, hence its name. The notes of the tritone divide an octave (particularly when conceptualized as twelve half tones of the chromatic scale) exactly into two equal parts. By raising the fourth degree of the scale or lowering the fifth degree of the eight-tone diatonic scale, the intervals of the perfect fourth and perfect fifth, respectively, are altered to achieve the tritone. Perfect fourths and fifths are considered stable intervals. The tritone is experienced as an unstable interval and our expectation demands resolution. The heard sound of the tritone is picked up by a listener with relatively little difficulty.

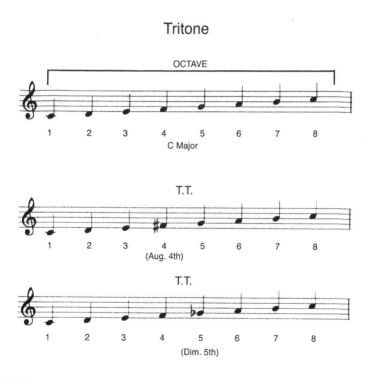

Figure 2.1 C major scale with tritone illustrated as augmented 4th and/or diminished 5th

The tritone has been considered the most ambiguous of all musical intervals since the sixteenth century. It is used as a prominent musical indicator for instability. Its sound is experienced as a strident dissonance that seeks tonal resolution, and thus it is a compositional and aural symbol of restless unease. The tritone is neither a major nor minor interval; it is an *altered* interval and is considered an imperfect fourth or fifth. (As mentioned earlier, in the diatonic scale, or octave, the intervals of the fourth and the fifth are considered "perfect" in the Western harmonic canon.)

The earliest known reference to the "tritonus" (Drabkin, 2001, quoted in The New Grove Dictionary of Music and Musicians, 2001, p. 748) was in the ninth or tenth century. In the thirteenth century, the tritone was called a "discordantia perfecta" (as were the dissonant intervals of the minor second and major seventh). Considered an "unstable interval" (Drabkin, 2001, in Groves, p. 748), it was nicknamed the "diabolus in musica" (i.e., the devil in music), a description that stuck until the end of the Renaissance. Its use was typically avoided by composers.

During the Baroque and Classical music eras, the tritone became an accepted compositional device. In Romantic and contemporary music, composers employed the tritone with even greater freedom, unencumbered by its satanic connotations. One way in which this interval was interwoven into a musical fabric was as a modulator to a distant key, which had the effect on the listener of aurally evoking a strong emotional reaction. By the twentieth century, particularly in twelve-tone and serial music, the tritone was considered a neutral interval and an important aspect of the overall structure of music composition.

Bernstein is in distinguished historical and contemporary company in his use of the tritone. Bach, Mozart, Beethoven, Mendelssohn, Liszt, Wagner, Debussy, Stravinsky, Bartók, Crumb, and many others have used the tritone both intervalically and thematically to create harmonic instability, restlessness, and emotional tension. The tritone features prominently in many jazz compositions and improvisations of the twentieth and twenty-first centuries as well.

Not to be underestimated affectively and musically is the historical significance of the shofar's blast at Mount Sinai, both to announce the Ten Commandments and to bring down the walls of Jericho. While the tones of the ram's horn are not identically those of the tritone, the spirit of the shofar's call is felt in the sound of the tritone that opens *West Side Story* and in this interval's various transformations throughout the musical. There is ample evidence in Bernstein's biographies that he wrestled with his Creator – both parental and godly – so it is inevitable that sonic impressions and memories of his early years would find their way consciously and unconsciously into his musical vocabulary. Bernstein's early years included a synagogue education, where he undoubtedly heard the sounds of the shofar – as well as the repeated insistence of his father, deaf to the his young son's prodigious talent and musical interests, to take over the family beauty supply business.[2]

We can appreciate the shofar's sound and its meaning – which encompasses battle and holy moments – in Bernstein's use of the tritone as a sonic signifier for the complexities that permeate the intrapsychic and interpersonal dynamics of the Caucasian Jets and the Puerto Rican Sharks. Bernstein was famous for his probing musical insights as well as for his verbal virtuosity with puns, anagrams, and neologisms. Although I do not believe that applying analytic concepts to a composer in absentia are particularly effective in analyzing his music, I nevertheless suggest that Bernstein's musical manipulation of the tritone throughout *West Side Story* can be likened to musical word play, leading to the speculation that the tritone was a multiply determined aural vehicle that allowed him to express his own intrapsychic contradictions through sound (Nagel, 2010a).

Beginning with the jarring trumpet blast of the tritone in the prologue (replaced by three whistles in the film version), which evokes the three traditional calls of the shofar, and on through its brilliant permutations in the entire score, this diabolical interval both forebodes and reflects unsettling musical themes, as well as intrapsychic and interpersonal complexities.[3] It is precisely the imperfect, enigmatic quality of the tritone that identifies ambiguity in the moods of the characters and the complex narratives throughout *West Side Story*. As listeners and viewers, we long for a consonant resolution of the tensions *between* the gangs and *within* their psyches. The constant presence of the tritone keeps us discordantly and dissonantly immersed in the world of the Sharks and the Jets, as well as in our own conscious and unconscious layers of intrapsychic and interpersonal warfare.

Leonard Bernstein's daughter, Jamie Bernstein, reflected on her relationship with her father and on his composition of *West Side Story* at a 2009 discussion group of which I am Chair at the American Psychoanalytic Association. Interestingly, she reported that her father commented he had not consciously used the tritone in the musical. Mark Eden Horowitz (personal communication, 2008), a senior librarian of the Bernstein Collection at the Library of Congress, indicated that once Bernstein realized he was drawn to the tritone, he developed it in the score. In Humphrey Burton's (1994) biography of the composer, Bernstein is quoted about the tritone that "pervades the whole piece … I didn't do all this on purpose. It seemed to come out in 'Cool' and the gang whistle in the Prologue" (p. 274).

An exploration of the great mystery of artistic creation is beyond the scope of this chapter. Yet it is fascinating to speculate about what a composer "means" when making particular musical choices that are expressed through the symbolism and metaphors of musical notation. Bernstein's own words about his use of the tritone provide a glimpse into his unconscious processes and their connection to creativity, since all mental activity begins in the unconscious. Yet we have musical clues – sonic evidence – with which to probe psychoanalytic concepts, associations, and affects. In studying and listening to a great musical masterpiece, we become aware of these as we explore what is evoked within us.

Frankly, I wonder how Bernstein could have used any *other* interval or musical gesture to so poignantly capture *in sound* the complexities and urgency of the intrapsychic and interpersonal dramas played out in *West Side Story*. The *diabolus in musica* expresses ambiguity as a leitmotif throughout *West Side Story*. Due to the tritone's musical construction, its harmonic instability, and multiple functions, the tritone in *West Side Story* repeatedly arouses the listener aurally and emotionally, whether or not he or she has any formal knowledge of music theory.[4] I concur with Pratt (1952, cited in Noy, 1993 in Feder *et al.*, 1993), who suggests that "music sounds as emotion feels" (p. 127), and also with the reviewer in the *Washington Post* who claimed that "Leonard Bernstein's music makes us feel what we do not understand" (Burton, 1994, p. 279).

"You pushed me": Affect becomes action

When Maria sings "I Feel Pretty," anticipating her reunion with Tony after the dance, the tritone is not used as a musical marker; her feelings are unambiguous. The music and rhythm of the gentle, off-the-beat cha-cha after she meets Tony at the dance contains the ominous interval, however. Later, Maria's dreamlike ballet with Tony, sans tritone, make the walls disappear as they join in a wishful, simple prayer-like song: "Somewhere . . . to find a new way of living, we'll find a way of forgiving . . . . Somewhere ... there's a place for us, a time and place of us. Hold my hand and we're halfway there. Hold my hand and I'll take you there. Somehow, some day, somewhere!" (vocal score, pp. 164–5). But this dream of Maria's and Tony's turns into a nightmare as their Romeo-and-Juliet balcony/fire escape erodes into the no-exit alleyway of aggression and violence.

In the play, the magnificent ensemble reprise of "Tonight" in Act One – compositionally rivaling both the famous sextet in Donizetti's *Lucia di Lammermoor* and the Quartet in Verdi's *Rigoletto* – anticipates three events: a fair fight between the Sharks and Jets (e.g., a fight without weapons), a forbidden romantic rendezvous for Maria and Tony, and steamy sex for Anita and Bernardo. The tritone as a musical marker is absent as each major character sings about what he or she anticipates later that evening. There is excitement, optimism, and energy in the air.

Not long after the ensemble concludes, we hear someone yell "You pushed me!" At this moment, the promise of a "fair fight," as well as Maria and Tony's hope for a future "far, far away, out of here," begins to explode and collapse. How quickly the steam of sexual energy can ignite into the fire of aggression. The ideals and longings on both sides, thus far expressed as edgy thoughts and affects, escalate rapidly into violent action as the dissonance between the Sharks and Jets erupts into open warfare.

Being and feeling pushed disturbs any brittle veneer of psychic equilibrium and anticipation – i.e., *mental constructs* – and propels the gangs instead into violence – i.e., *action*. With their honor threatened, the Jets' and Sharks' bravado ceases to contain their humiliation, hopelessness, and increasing detachment from internal or external constraints. The sentiments expressed in Maria and Tony's "Tonight" duet are dashed. Fragile compromise formations that have barely contained aggressive impulses underlying shame, despair, and rage boil over into mayhem. The psyches of the Sharks and Jets hang precariously on a narcissistic cliff between illusions of omnipotence and humiliating disgrace; their vengefulness wards off unbearable shame (Lansky, 2007b, c).

During the melee, Bernardo kills Riff and Tony kills Bernardo. The fair fight unexpectedly turns foul. The tritone is orchestrated into the fabric of the score as the action culminates in a double murder.

Dear Officer Krupke

By this time in *West Side Story*, we have become well acquainted aurally, compositionally, and emotionally with the *diabolus in musica*. We have witnessed the Jets and Sharks boasting, bragging, taunting. In the inflammatory chaos of their "fair" fight, knives flash and instincts are ignited. Something, somewhere has gone dreadfully wrong to create these bright, restless, and emotionally impoverished young men, who, in trying to find a better life in the teeming hotbed of New York City streets, begin to boil over with revenge and fury.

As simmering emotional and musical tensions reach their dramatic climax, Bernstein offers the song "Gee! Officer Krupke," as the Jets try to explain the roots of their psychological and social distress to themselves and to their buddy, who mimics a blustering policeman, Officer Krupke. In each stanza and refrain, they maintain that they have "gone bad" because adults do not understand them. While the clever, catchy lyrics command attention, the music powerfully conveys the bitter irony and ambiguity beneath their bravado. This rollicking circus parody of psycho-sexual-social development gone awry is a musical testament to the power of early attachments, narcissistic injuries, castration fears, challenged compromise formations, social prejudice, and the affects of shame, humiliation, hate, and rage. As we have witnessed, this swirling mixture has propelled thoughts and affects into aggressive assault.

Throughout this jaunty song, the unstable tritone reminds us repeatedly of the paradoxes and complexities in this engaging but also quite sobering music. The tritone aurally exposes the Jets' manifest boldness and latent anxiety as it ominously reappears before each stanza; the interval is first sung on the words, "Dear ... kindly" (E sharp to B in the key of B major). It is a sonic, sarcastic, verbal, and musical attack on all types of authority. The tritone accentuates the Jets' boisterous, sardonic psychological explanations, their pseudo-confessions, and their abundant externalizations.

Paralleling their fluctuating good/bad self-assessments and their narcissistic and competitive vulnerabilities, their catchy refrain zigzags through various musical modulations. Of note, in the first stanza the key of

B major modulates to a key that is a tritone's distance away: that of F major. The ambiguity of the *diabolus in musica* allows the Jets to simultaneously both mock and fear Officer Krupke – who, patrolling the streets silently like an absent parent, represents the family, society, egos, and superegos that have failed them. The Jets insightfully describe how their psychic seeds were sown in earliest childhood and maintain that they are imprisoned in their cultural surround.

Gee, Officer Krupke
Jets

Figure 2.2 The tritone – E sharp to B natural

"I didn't get the love that ev'ry child ought-a get": the illusion and disillusionment of omnipotence

The Jet A-rab caustically describes his friend, ingeniously named Action, to Officer Krupke – his superego proxy and absent parent – explaining that "society's played him a terrible trick" (vocal score, p. 182). The Jets gleefully and provocatively recount that "We never had the love that ev'ry child ought-a get" (vocal score, p. 173). They struggle with the notion that "We ain't no delinquents, we're misunderstood. Deep down inside of us there is good!" (vocal score, pp. 173–4). Their projections and fledgling egos and superegos are heard in Bernstein's music as he employs a *plagal cadence* (a chord progression familiar in church hymns, also known as the "Amen" cadence – harmonically, the IV-I cadence). When the Jets declare "there is good" about themselves, their words are sung on the plagal cadence (vocal score, p. 174).

Action: Deep down inside us there is good!
Action: There is good! [*Plagal cadence: E major (IV chord) resolves to B Major (I chord)*]
Jets: There is good, there is untapped good. Like inside, the worst of us is good!

(vocal score, pp. 174–5)

Figure 2.3 Plagal cadence

An altered plagal cadence is heard in a subsequent verse when another gang member, Baby John, by this time accepting the mantle that the Jets are "bad," asserts that "it ain't just a question of misunderstood – deep down inside him, he's no good!" (vocal score, p. 186). Action seconds his claim: "I'm no good" (vocal score, p. 186). This time Bernstein modifies the plagal cadence as he turns the IV chord in D major into a G minor chord, instead of a G major chord. By lowering the third degree in the G major chord to make it minor, Bernstein musically underscores the impact of lowered self-esteem expressed in the lyrics.

Baby John: "Deep down inside him, he's no good!"
Action: "I'm no good!" [*Here there is an altered plagal cadence: the G minor chord (IV with a lowered third degree) resolves to a D major (I) chord; vocal score, p. 186*]
Jets: "We're no good, we're no earthly good, like the best of us is no damn good!"

(vocal score, pp. 186–7)

Figure 2.4 Plagal cadence with lowered 3rd degree in first chord

Should the lyrics somehow not convince the listener about the parody, poignancy, and ambiguity here, the music conveys the message.

Finally, as though in church, the Jets kneel to lampoon prayer (and their lack of redemption):

> "Gee, Officer Krupke, we're down on our knees, 'cause no one wants a fellow with a social disease!"
>
> (vocal score, pp. 189–90)

The tritone is first heard in the opening of "Gee, Officer Krupke" in the key of B major, on E sharp (a raised fourth) /F natural (a lowered fifth). Once this tritone settles into the key of F major – a key that is a tritone away (i.e., the tonal center that concludes the song) – the Jets "Krup" the officer and return to their prison of low self-esteem. Bernstein's treatment of the tritone as an interval, as a modulation, and as the tonal center at the conclusion of this rousing number is musically akin to what psychoanalysts would refer to as overdetermination, displacement, and/or multiple function.

The Jets' shame and humiliation are emphasized in their vocal reprisals anchored in their intrapsychic dynamics and social ostracism. The "good" that is deep inside of them is tragically unacknowledged by those like Office Krupke who could help them, but instead stand by idly. Officer Schrank, too, relentlessly insults and verbally abuses them – as they do to themselves and to each other. One can only begin to imagine what has occurred in their childhoods.

While the Jets have reason to mistrust and hate, they have also become victims of their hardened sense of injustice, so that that they are unable to "find a way of forgiving" (vocal score, p. 164) the outcome envisioned by Tony and Maria. As the Jets parade and parody their insights about the origins of their predicament, it is Bernstein's inspired use of the tritone that musically reminds us of the tenacity of inner tensions and frustrated longings for love and acceptance that are fueled by parental failures (Lansky, 1992), inept social institutions, and cultural prejudice. All of these factors contribute to block self-respect and are sonically represented by the presence of the *diabolus in musica* – which, ironically, reappears musically on the affectionate word *dear*.

Painful affects and human dilemmas do not disappear beneath restless musical modulations and rollicking sarcasm in "Gee, Officer Krupke." The caustic wit and manifest levity in Bernstein's music do not promote greater insight for the Jets and Sharks, or greater tolerance from authority figures (such as the police officers and parents) who are in a position to help them. Separated by diverse cultures, deep down inside, the Jets and Sharks are remarkably alike.

In "Gee! Officer Krupke," the Puerto Rican and Caucasian gangs exemplify the psychoanalytic concepts of projection and splitting, employed to shield their shame, castration fears, and defended but depleted self-regard (Lansky, 2007b, c; Nagel, 2008b). The acts of winning turf wars and ruling their alleyways feed their narcissistic illusions of omnipotence and power. Long out of tune with caregivers, the Jets and Sharks display their pseudo-supremacy and inability to forgive (Lansky, 2005, 2007b, c; Smith 2008). The magical thinking that cradles their vulnerability resonates with hostility and prevents "redemption through accountability" (Zizek, 2009, p. 81), through which they would have been able to grant themselves forgiveness.

In the character of frightened Baby John, we see a glimmer of ambivalence that is manifestly avoided by the tough guys. Another "outsider" is the asexual character Anybodys, who longs to be one of the "juvenile delinquents." These two characters introduce a homosexual element into the narrative, but even more so, they underscore the poignant need to belong and to feel appreciated – a theme shared by Anybodys and everybody.

The gangs have convinced themselves that they exercise power on the West Side streets through intimidation and successful fighting, whenever they feel unheard, misunderstood, unloved, or threatened. The call of the tritone beneath the word *dear* in each stanza of "Gee! Officer Krupke" communicates the Jets' and Sharks' longing for love and their cries of despair, which are defensively encrusted in shame, hardened cynicism, and hate. (In the third stanza, the word *my* is sung on the tritone instead of *dear,* which appears every other time the tritone begins a stanza.) A term of endearment, *dear,* combined with a diabolical musical interval embedded in a cancan-style patter song, highlights the bitter irony and ambiguity of the tritone and the unresolved pathos of the gangs. The Jets are convinced that neither Officer Krupke nor anyone else has ever listened to them or ever will (despite the character Doc's attempts to do so).

For both the Jets and Sharks, selfhood is under attack continually. It is all the more heartbreaking when Tony, trying to find something better "someday, somehow, somewhere," falls prey to a fair fight gone foul when he kills Bernardo.

The Sharks' and Jets' affects and actions raise complex questions about projections and splitting, jealousy, and envy. To forgive[5] one another and to not react viscerally to feeling "pushed around" could be experienced as complicity with their betrayers, both current and past. Psychically imprisoned by early trauma, the Jets issue a message of ridicule and insight to convey "double identifications with both aggressor and victim" as their "legitimate self-assertion [was] in short supply" (Cooper, 2005, p. 129). Manifestly, the music and lyrics of "Gee, Officer Krupke" temporarily relieve the tension and devastation that have accumulated in *West Side Story,* permitting us to catch our breath – or at least gasp – until the next major plot twist: Anita, who is trying to save the lovers but is not immune to relentless humiliation and attempted rape by the Jets at Doc's shop, tells a lie and betrays Maria by saying Maria has been killed by Chino. Disoriented and overwhelmed by his grief, Tony runs into the street and is killed by Chino just as he catches sight of Maria. As *West Side Story* draws to its anguished conclusion, with Tony dying in Maria's arms, the strains of "Somewhere" are indeed far away.

Somehow ... Someday ... Somewhere

Moving ahead (even though prejudice and alienation continue to be with us today, as when the musical was written), in both 1957 and its 2009 revival, the Sharks and Jets display a "powerful share of aggressiveness" on the West Side streets of New York, and they defend themselves when they feel attacked from without and from within. In this respect, the creators of *West Side Story* are in concert with Freud as they convey through words, music, and action the complex social, ethnic, and psychic pulse of young gang members who become metaphors for what each of us may also experience "deep down inside us" (to again quote the lyrics from "Gee, Officer Krupke").

Indeed, as the Jets explain – through the sound of the tritone – to the "dear" officer, they *do* have a "social [and psychological] *dis-ease.*" They are also looking for a "cure" for their maladies, yet no one listens or understands (Officer Krupke exemplifies the attitude of others). The narrative of *West Side Story* and the ambiguity of the tritone transcend the proscenium of the stage, as well as any given historical moment. The message of the tritone's call throughout *West Side Story* begs for recognition, understanding, and attention to the consequences of unattended psychic and social distress.

I maintain that we should bring the "couch" – i.e., psychoanalytically informed theories of mental functioning – to educators, community organizations, social service agencies, and police departments, to assist them in their social, educational, and emotional engagements with young people at risk from physical and emotional harm. As *West Side Story* illustrates, this vulnerable population, when provoked and/or ignored, is liable to turn mentation into action because they "didn't get the love ev'ry child ought-a get."

Bernstein's use of the tritone in *West Side Story* not only sonically emphasizes the ambiguity and complexity inherent in all mental functioning, but also uses the *diabolus in musica* as a "war"-ning siren for all Officer Krupkes and others who patrol streets and minds where "powerful destructive forces continue to threaten the survival of humanity" (Tylim, 2009, p. 97). Is it too far-fetched to envision that someday the verses of "Gee, Officer Krupke" may be introduced with musical notes other than the *diabolus in musica,* and that somewhere there could really be a safe place for Marias and Tonys?

It seems that Freud may not have known *why* he felt moved by certain pieces of music (Cheshire, 1996; Nagel, 2007, 2008a; Barale and Minazzi, 2008). Interestingly, his comments about it (see Part I), rather than being dismissive of music altogether, suggest that he rebelled against it precisely because he did not understand how or why it affected him. In what manner Freud was sensitive to the sonic sphere and to "unheard melodies" (Keats, cited in Lombardi, 2008, p. 1191) remains as unclear today as his disclaimer continues to ring paradoxical.

It is my fantasy that Freud would have resonated to the music in *West Side Story* and the aural (oral) significance of the ambiguity inherent in the tritone – even if he did not fully understand the music and his own reaction. Leonard Bernstein's personal philosophy, expressed here through his musical vocabulary, underlies his attempt to define through sound the discontent of invisible enemies who inhabit the psyches of the Jets and Sharks. He well understood that these enemies from within and without threaten "gentile creatures who want to be loved" (Freud, 1930, p. 111), and his music illustrates how difficult it is to make them obsolete (Oja and Horowitz, 2008).

From a psychoanalytic point of view, Lombardi proposes that associations to music "bridge the gap between the concrete and the abstract, body and mind, the nonsymbolic and the symbolic, as well as between internal and the external" (2008, p. 1199). These functions assist in organizing presymbolic emotions and mental functioning – both in clinical work and in our appreciation of music. Bernstein's compositional choices, conscious and unconscious – such as use of the tritone leitmotif in *West Side Story* – provide sonic evidence that musical data can illuminate psychoanalytic concepts and contribute to the organization of psychic processes that are not easily accessible through words. Music, as another instrument in the applied/interdisciplinary psychoanalytic repertoire can, as I believe it does in *West Side Story,* "illuminate elements of the underlying structures of the mind" (Feder, 1993b, p. 4).

Bernstein's sensitivity to the ambiguity and tension inherent in the tritone in *West Side Story* can be conceptualized as an intersection among music theory and theories of mind, which carries implications for clinical practice. Transporting psychoanalytic concepts from the analytic couch to the Broadway stage and on into the community to address the complexities of love, aggression, violence, and prejudice is an exciting possibility. The concepts that link music with psychoanalysis have relevant implications for clinical practice as well as for interdisciplinary applications: how do we tune in and how are we moved by what we hear? Keeping this bridge between psychoanalysis and music in mind may assist us in helping patients with affect recognition, expression, and regulation, and, in certain situations, in containing emotions before they escalate into undesirable and/or violent actions (such as occurs between the Jets and Sharks).

The tritone in *West Side Story* musically deconstructs the psychoanalytic concept of splitting, i.e., the reductionistic notion of an "either/or" dichotomy regarding Puerto Rican/Caucasian, good/bad, cool/hot, love/hate. The ambiguity of the tritone sonically and thematically both widens and narrows the gap between "us" and "them," between preoedipal and oedipal dynamics, between affect and action, and between revenge and forgiveness, as it aurally conveys a continuum of elevating and disquieting dynamics that we all share – including the capacities for love, understanding, prejudice, hatred, revenge, and violence. The Sharks, Jets, and the *diabolus in musica* in *West Side Story* bring us compellingly close to the challenges posed by our own invisible enemies.

The tritone makes its final appearance as the concluding note (F sharp) in *West Side Story*. Maria cradles Tony in her arms as he dies; the music hovers around the tonality of E major, and the interval of a major second in the key of E is heard on F sharp. The notes evoke the memory of the song "Somewhere." An *ostinato* (i.e., a repeated note) on E anchors this tonality, until the E moves to F sharp (as mentioned, the second degree of the scale of E major). Choosing not to remain harmonically in the key of E, Bernstein moves the tonality to C major for the final four measures, holding onto the F sharp in the lower strings (cellos and double basses). Thus, the F sharp now becomes a tritone (an augmented fourth) in the key of C. The F sharp is played four times and concludes *West Side Story*.

We feel anguish through the throbbing presence of this final tritone. Yet its sonic ambiguity leaves open the possibility of grieving, of mourning, of finding "a way of forgiving," and of working through the invisible enemy of hatred for self and other –"Somehow … Someday … Somewhere."

Chapter 3

Case-ette 2

Self-esteem – *Peter and the Wolf*

Composers have used animals in their compositions, both in titles and in musically programmatic material. An examination of Sergei Prokofiev's musical fairy tale *Peter and the Wolf* emphasizes the development of musical thematic motifs that are counterpoint to Peter's psychosocial development, displaced onto animals and their adventures.

Music, dreams, and fairy tales

It has been suggested that musical structure is "analogous to the dream, daydream or joke" and can be "analyzed by psychoanalytic techniques to reveal its latent content" (Noy, 1967b, p. 45; see also Van der Chijs, 1923, 1926). In connecting musical expression to affect, Monsonyi (1935) highlights the "wish to play again like a child" (Noy, 1967b, p. 51). The notion of play, a hallmark of ego mastery, is ubiquitous in the structure of fairy tales. Play for children represents attempts to create order, to understand, and to master the psychological tasks of growing up. Although Bettelheim (1989) noted that "there is as yet no systematic discussion of fairy tales from a psychoanalytic viewpoint," (p. 313) he also stated:

> Applying the psychoanalytic model of the human personality, fairy tales carry important messages to the conscious, the preconscious, and the unconscious mind, on whatever level each is functioning at the time. By dealing with universal human problems, particularly those which preoccupy the child's mind, these stories speak to his budding ego and encourage its development, while at the same time relieving preconscious and unconscious pressures. As the stories unfold, they give conscious credence and body to id pressures and show ways to satisfy these that are in line with ego and superego requirements.
>
> (1989, p. 6)

Through the use of analogy and metaphor in fairy tales, characters are typically defined as embodying the opposite traits of good and evil. This apparently clear-cut duality presents a more nuanced task for the reader and listener, since evil is often seductive as well as dangerous, and good intentions can frequently lead to trouble. The wicked witch, the evil stepmother, and the devouring wolf all entice heroes, heroines, and young listeners as they simultaneously terrorize them. For example, in "The Three Little Pigs," the wolf is the vicious enemy from without who huffs and puffs, but he is also the enemy within – an externalization of the child's perceived badness – who represents "all asocial, unconscious, devouring powers against which one must learn to protect oneself, and which one can defeat through the strength of one's ego" (Bettelheim, p. 42).

In fairy tales, internal conflicts associated with growing up are often depicted by animals with whom the child can identify. As such they can represent different parts of his or her personality and allow the child to tackle difficult, contradictory, multiply determined intrapsychic and interpersonal tasks. It is not unusual for an evil motif to appear in the form of a dangerous animal that threatens to devour the hero (sometimes also an animal), who typically outsmarts and conquers the villain.

Music, animals, and psychoanalysis

Music can be programmatic in that melodies and musical motifs can represent affects as well as characters – as exemplified in Humperdinck's *Hansel and Gretel* and Strauss's *Til Eulenspeigel*. From a psychoanalytic perspective, animals, and by extension their musical representation in fairy tales, can be conceptualized as metaphors for consonances, dissonances, and for multiply determined conflicts and their potential resolutions through musical forms and harmonic structures.

Bettelheim (1989) suggests that the symbols and characters in fairy tales often parallel Freud's tripartite structural model of the *id, ego,* and *superego*. The wolf is a central character in two famous fairy tales, "The Three Little Pigs" and "Little Red Riding Hood." In this structural theoretical context (and surely in other models of the mind), the wild animal represents the instinctual drives, and these two stories illustrate how the ego and superego attempt to master sexual and aggressive dangers.

The wolf and other animals serve similar functions in Sergei Prokofiev's (1891–1953) musical fairy tale *Peter and the Wolf*. In this story (in which both libretto and music were written by the composer), literary and musical themes merge to depict themes of temptation, sexuality, evil, aggression, and mastery during the young protagonist's journey toward individuation, as narcissistic omnipotence and oedipal conflicts are gradually resolved. Upon closer examination of *Peter and the Wolf*, we appreciate that both music and psychoanalytic concepts inform and enhance the intrapsychic significance of the animals in this work and the development of its musical motifs.

Peter and the Wolf was begun in 1935, while Prokofiev was working on his ballet *Romeo and Juliet*. It was written during a period when some of his other compositions also had childlike titles and appeal (e.g., *The Ugly Duckling,* 1914; *The Love for Three Oranges,* 1919; *Music for Children* [for piano, 1935, and its orchestral version *Summer Day,* 1941]; *Cinderella,* 1940–44; and *The Tale of the Stone Flower,* 1948–53). *Peter and the Wolf* was composed after Prokofiev's return to Russia following almost twenty years of living in the West. Influenced by Soviet ideology as it developed following the Revolution – an ideology that fostered programmatic musical compositions favorable to the state – it is no accident that Prokofiev's main character in the score has the Russian name of "'Pioneer Petya,' a registered member of the Communist Youth Movement" (cited in the preface to the score of *Peter and the Wolf,* p. v). Nor is it surprising that Prokofiev's travels away from his homeland (or away from the garden, in his composition) and the composition of this piece are quite possibly reflected autobiographically in the parallel drama of the score and libretto. Psychological and musical themes weave contrapuntally with political, social, and cultural overtones in this composition beloved by children of all ages.

Prokofiev casts *Peter and the Wolf* as a composition in which the characters, both animal and human, are associated with particular musical instruments and tuneful themes. When asked about the possibility of having the flute represent a bird, the composer replied, "Of course we shall have the flute as a little bird. It is not a question of influencing the simple ideas of the children. The main thing is to find a common language" (Schlifstein, 1965, p. 480).

As Prokofiev set the orchestration, the boy Peter was represented by greater instrumental complexity than the other characters. For example, while each animal is identified by a melody played by a single instrument, Peter is initially introduced by a string quartet, with its full capacity for counterpoint. Further, the cast of human and animal characters possess particular attributes. The composer is quoted as saying, "Yes, it must all arise from the concrete, from opposites and from impressions: wolf-bird, bad-good, big-small. Sharply contrasting characters must have correspondingly contrasting sound-colours, and every role must have its leit-motiv" (Schlifstein, 1965, p. 480). This intentional creation of polarities makes the complexities of mental life more accessible for the young mind, in which splitting is a developmental phenomenon. However, the broad and lasting impact of this composition underscores that this music, with its psychological underpinnings, is not appreciated exclusively by the child, nor is it split into either/or polarities.

Musically, the score is conceived in three connected sections. The instruments are introduced verbally by a narrator before the composition begins, and then again musically in the exposition. Characters/instruments are presented in the following order: Peter (string quartet), bird (flute), duck (oboe), cat (clarinet), grandfather (bassoon), the wolf (horns), and the hunters with their guns (tympani).

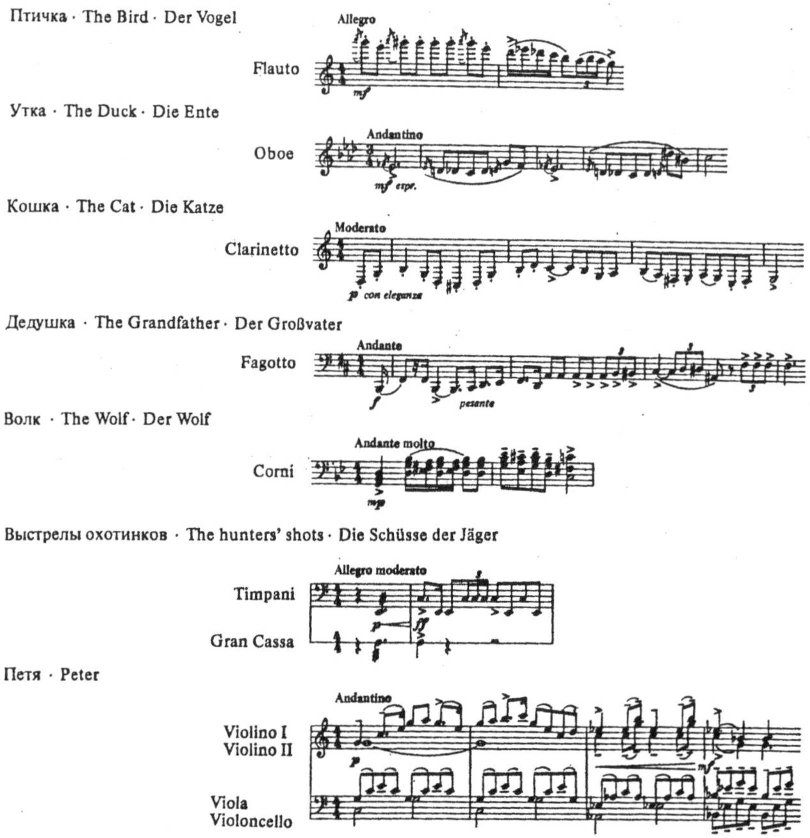

Figure 3.1 The musical instruments that identify the animals and musical themes in *Peter and the Wolf*

Compositionally, the dramatic climax occurs during the second section, when a menacing gray wolf appears, terrorizes Peter and the frolicking animals, and swallows the duck. A hint of disharmony and conflict appears earlier in the score as the cat tries to catch the bird while they play in the meadow. The hunters, with their guns, also appear in the development section, although Peter has already caught the wolf by the time they arrive.

The recapitulation, or third and concluding section, exults in taking the wolf to the zoo in a triumphant procession. Of note is the recapitulation of Peter's musical theme: here the music is transformed from its original simple, uncomplicated opening melody played by string-quartet instruments into a stately, full orchestral march as all the animals (but one) exuberantly join the parade.

Prokofiev completed his composition in one week, with an additional seven days necessary for its orchestration. Before its premier, the composer informally played *Peter and the Wolf* on the piano for some children. Their response led him to perform the concluding triumphal march three times. The first complete performance took place on May 2, 1936, at the Central Children's Theater in Moscow. Success was immediate. Quoted in the 1985 Eulenberg orchestral score is a letter from a ten-year-old boy who had attended a performance; this letter illustrates the boy's pleasure and identification with the musical story: "What I liked best was the way Peter struggled with the wolf and the way all the instruments played as the wolf was beaten and led away to the zoo" (p. ix[1]).

Ostensibly for children, *Peter and the Wolf* reveals much about the intrapsychic life shared by people of all ages. A narrator begins the piece as follows: "Early one morning young Peter opened the garden gate, and went out into the big green meadow" (p. 1). A string quartet plays Peter's theme in C major, a simple key with a tranquil, skipping sort of melody centered round dotted eighth and sixteenth notes. The aural message conveys the image of a carefree, innocent, and adventurous young boy going outside to play. The green meadow is beckoning and the mood is idyllic, conjuring up a mental picture of the Garden of Eden.

Peter's animal friends appear, beginning with a little bird "high up in a tree .... Everything is quiet and still, the little bird chirps merrily" (p. 3). Shortly afterward the flute plays its bird theme, melodically defined by grace notes and closer intervals than in Peter's lilting motif. A duet ensues between the bird's music and Peter's music. As the two interact, one might conjecture that the bird represents a part of Peter's innocence, whose greenness, like the fresh meadow, is portrayed by a simple melody that contrasts with his adventuresome spirit, indicated by the wider intervals (spaces between the notes) of his melody.

Yet Peter is about to explore the larger world beyond the gate – while leaving the entrance open. A female duck appears, who "is glad that Peter hasn't shut the garden gate and she decides to take a bath in the deep pond in the meadow" (p. 6). The oboe characterizes this feathered friend in a lower register than the flute (the bird), and with a key change hinting that the simple material of the opening might become more complex – which indeed it does. We recall that Peter did not shut the garden gate, and we now hear that the duck, too, has noted this. One musical and programmatic implication here is that change (instrumental and intrapsychic change) – perhaps trouble – is anticipated. Moreover, the duck metaphorically represents the part of Peter that can regress to the perceived safety of his childhood should separation prove too overwhelming.

The narrator then proceeds to tell us that the duck is "bathing" in the pond, not merely swimming, in deep water (Who is dirty? Is Peter or the duck doing or thinking something forbidden – or are they getting into water over their heads?). Since the depth of water is immaterial to an animal who can swim (just as a gate is irrelevant to a bird who can fly), the latent message here is that Peter, like the duck, may get into deep trouble (or deep water) in venturing beyond the gate.

Also, we realize that the lake is the animals' domain; Peter cannot go into it as the duck can. Generational and sexual boundaries are suggested in this child-and-animal scene. The skipping musical intervals and cheery nature of Peter's opening musical motif are now augmented by the chromatic and somber musical statement of the duck. Soon the bird and duck began to taunt each other about their respective potency: "What sort of bird are you, when you can't even fly, he [the bird] said? And what sort of bird are you, the duck retorted, when you can't even swim? And she flopped in the pond" (p. 8).

We might conceptualize these arguing birds as conflicting elements emerging from within Peter. The musical duet, with its alternation of the high, fluttering bird theme with darker, slinking duck music, evokes a psychic counterpoint in Peter's capacity for mastery: will he sink or swim as he asserts his autonomy and initiative in the meadow? Can he really remain innocent and as "green" as the meadow once he has "opened the garden gate"? The musical duet between the two feathered animals (both of whom can fly, but one of whom chooses not to, stubbornly flopping in the water) aurally portrays an intrapsychic dilemma. Leaving home is attractive, dangerous, and necessary for Peter, just as it is for Hansel and Gretel, and for Little Red Riding Hood, in order to master the contradictory elements "residing in … [the self] and the world" (Bettelheim, 1989, p. 182).

As the duck and bird argue, "Peter has a sudden fright. Creeping stealthily toward them, through the grass, comes a cat" (p. 11). Her presence is announced by the clarinet in a low, sinister-sounding register whose steady rhythm is the opposite of Peter's dotted rhythm. Things at once become more ominous in the garden. The cat, doing what comes instinctively, has designs on the duck and the bird, and plots to catch the bird as the latter argues with the duck. "'So the bird is busy with his quarrel? I'll soon catch him!' And without a sound, on velvet paws, she crept up towards him" (p. 12).

Seduction, secrecy, and danger are personified in this female feline who stalks the bird. This predator "on velvet paws" implies that dangers lurk around us and that innocence can be lost without warning; that which is quiet, soft, and pleasurable can also be dangerous.

The music quickens as Peter realizes what is happening and yells "watch out" (p. 13) to the bird, who flies into a tree. During this musically dramatic episode, the duck squawks at the cat from the pond but does not fly to safety. Of interest musically and psychoanalytically, the duck's squawking is actually performed by the string quartet, which is Peter's musical signature. This transformation in orchestration is congruent with the earlier hypothesis that Prokofiev is musically developing the animals as externalizations of Peter's inner struggles.

While the cat is plotting mischief, we learn for the first time that Peter himself was being disobedient when he set out to explore the garden. The bassoon, the lowest ranged instrument of all those in this composition, introduces Peter's grandfather in heavy, deep-register dotted rhythms (contrasting with Peter's buoyant dotted rhythms of the opening). He scolds Peter because "he was angry with Peter for going out of the garden gate. It's dangerous out here: what would happen if a wolf came out of the woods? What then?" (p. 16).

Peter had not paid attention to this warning; he "explained that boys like him were not afraid of wolves" (p. 19). Peter's disobedience, fueled by his sense of omnipotence, his curiosity about the world, and his feelings of invincibility, led him to disregard his grandfather's warning. Although the music gaily skips around – Peter's theme is heard once more in the strings, reminiscent of the opening scene in the garden – this time his music is doubled by the clarinet, the cat's instrument. It is at this point, both in the score and in the story, that Peter demonstrates his fearlessness while also musically suggesting his identification with the "troublemakers" in the garden. Since we know the garden gate had not been closed, regression to the safe, gratifying (yet restrictive) parental home (or Peter's internalization of it) is available in times of inner chaos. Grandfather "took Peter by the hand, led him home, and firmly locked the gate behind them" (p. 20). A unison *portato* (accented) scale descends to a *forte* (loud) chordal cadence.

At this point, the music and the libretto bring into focus some of the intrapsychic conflicts that children experience as they grow up and leave home. The grandfather, multiply determined as a sexual and generational oedipal rival, as well as a superego metaphor, has been internalized as both a good and parental introject and a restrictive one; he saves Peter from internal and external dangers while also preventing him from exerting his potency beyond the garden gate.

For now Peter appears safe, but all is not safe. "And indeed, no sooner had Peter gone than out of the woods came an enormous grey wolf" (p. 21). The wolf's musical theme is announced by a crescendo of chorale-like chords played by three horns. A *tremolo* (quivering) is heard in the other instruments, and the musical message clearly conveys to the listener that serious trouble has arrived in the meadow. The trembling animals scurry to take cover: "the cat shot up into the tree" (p. 23); her music quickens from eighth notes to triplets to grace notes, portraying the panic she experiences. "The duck squawked and fluttered and quickly got out of the pond" (p. 24), but "flap as she might, the wolf was faster .... He got closer ... and closer" (pp. 24–5). We hear the music recommence first with the oboe (the duck) and then with the flute (the bird), and the latter is doubled by the first violin in a string quartet. As the action and affects intensify, the flute, oboe, clarinet, and string quartet all culminate in *fortissimo* (very loud) sound, and we are told by the narrator that "he [the wolf] caught up with her [the duck] ... seized her ... and swallowed her up" (p. 25).

A *fermata* (a musical symbol telling the musicians to hold a note or a rest longer than its rhythmic value) over a whole-note rest brings the score to a screeching but silent halt. This lengthy pause emphasizes the unspeakable gravity of what has just happened; the absence of sound represents the ultimate anxiety of nonbeing. Still unsatisfied, "the wolf was pacing around the tree, looking up at them [the cat and the bird] with greedy eyes" (p. 28).

"Meanwhile, Peter had been standing behind the locked gate and had seen all that had happened without being at all afraid" (p. 29). Peter's theme is now presented by the quartet *and* the clarinet (the latter being the cat's signature instrument). The cat's instrumentation combined with Peter's suggests greater intrapsychic complexity for Peter. Peter devises a scheme to capture the wolf (and his own devouring impulses), climbing into the tree with the bird and enlisting its aid. They work together to lower a lasso to snare the wolf, as the flute and string quartet alternate in bringing Peter's theme to life. Yet the bird, who has been entrusted with lowering the rope around the wolf while Peter holds it from up in the tree, "almost brushed the wolf's muzzle with his wings, and the wolf sprang angrily at him, this way and that" (p. 33).

We learn from the narrator "how the little bird teased the wolf! And how the wolf longed to catch hold of him! But the little bird was cunning, and the wolf just couldn't catch him" (p. 35). The excitement of this rescue mission mixes pleasure with danger, delight with fear, until finally Peter achieves victory; he "made a noose with his rope, and very carefully he lowered it down …. He slipped the noose over the wolf's tail and pulled it tight" (pp. 36–7). The wolf struggled mightily, but "the leaps of the wolf only drew the noose tighter around his tail" (p. 41), until Peter emerges triumphant.

In defying his grandfather to venture forth, witnessing a stimulating scene from behind the gate, flirting with temptation that was both dangerous and desirous, and lassoing the wolf, Peter crossed a threshold from innocent child to initiated hero. Like the children in "Hansel and Gretel" who pushed the witch into the oven, Peter can now be rid of the "persecuting figures of his imagination" (Bettelheim, 1989, p. 166). In the process, he comes to realize that he possesses sexual potency within himself, as well as the cunning, destructive, and devouring qualities of the wolf.

When the hunters appear in the meadow firing their guns, orchestrated as tympani, Peter and the little bird have already saved the day through resourcefulness and collaboration. Peter announces, "You don't need to shoot. The little bird and I have already caught the wolf. Help us take him off to the zoo" (p. 48). Peter now relies less on externalization as he transports (or expels) the wolf part of himself, still alive, to the zoo. Peter has tamed his multiply determined inner forces, which he can now use adaptively in the service of competence and pleasure, as evidenced by his leadership of the triumphant procession.

Peter's personal transformation is paralleled by a musical transformation in thirty-three bars of the score, as the meter shifts from a 4/4 to a 3/4 time signature, and the tonality modulates first to A flat major and then to E major.

Peter's theme becomes more lilting and more embellished than the simpler one that previously identified him. Even the tempo marking for the opening presentation of his theme, *andantino,* is now altered to *andante;* the diminutive *ino* is removed.

By the time we approach the end of the score, Peter has experienced and incorporated many mental transformations. The wolf he has encountered is similar to the one in "Little Red Riding Hood," in which

> The wolf is the externalization of the badness the child feels when he goes contrary to the admonitions of his parents and permits himself to tempt, or to be tempted, sexually. When he strays from the path his parent has outlined for him, he encounters "badness" and he fears that it will swallow up him and the parent whose confidence he betrayed.
>
> (Bettelheim, 1989, p. 177)

Indeed, Peter's intrapsychic and interpersonal growth allows him to march forth triumphantly. In the march that concludes the composition, we hear all the animal themes recapitulated, with Peter's string quartet now fully orchestrated. Peter's melody is performed expansively by the horns – the wolf's identifying instruments – but with quarter notes and dotted eighth notes – an augmentation of Peter's rhythm. This augmentation of Peter's original theme in dotted eighth and sixteenth notes, first played by four strings, utilizes a musical vocabulary to further illustrate Peter's arrival at a new level of psychic integration.

Yet ever present is the warning offered by the cautious (or envious?) grandfather, who is unable to fully acknowledge Peter's potency, "Well well. But what if Peter hadn't caught the wolf? What then?" (p. 60). Fragments of Grandfather's theme are heard alternating with the cat's music played on the clarinet, as caution and temptation, age and youth, are musically paired. The little bird, Peter's companion, nevertheless chirps merrily in the glow of ego mastery: "See how clever we are, Peter and I! See what we have caught!" (p. 66).

Despite the happy conclusion, *Peter and the Wolf* ends with ambiguity as we learn that "If you listened carefully, you could hear the duck, still quacking inside the wolf. For the wolf had been in such a hurry that he had swallowed her alive" (p. 68). The duck, a female, is split off from Peter's male identity and seems to be residing inside the wolf's belly, having been swallowed whole. But although she is alive and still quacking, we ponder: has she truly been saved – will she get out … or ultimately die inside the wolf? Ambiguity, gender identity, and fantasy abound in the midst of psychic growth and triumph. The wolf's belly is both a haven from danger and a danger in itself. Fantasies of pregnancy and birth (and death) are implicated in this incomplete resolution of the story.

And what about good and evil, justice and injustice? The wolf survives despite his oral greed, while the unsuspecting duck has been traumatized and may not live. What lessons will young listeners and older ones take with them from this musical story that is rich with psychoanalytic themes? Each listener will resolve such dilemmas in a personally meaningful way.

In an autobiographical association, I recall one of my theory teachers at The Juilliard School, Hugh Aitken, who repeatedly emphasized the "heard" sound of a musical composition, rather than merely focusing on its technical analysis. Importance was placed on what the music actually sounded like, regardless of what a theory book said it *should* sound like. Listening was an experiential and meaningful experience, as a counterpoint to the study of theory and formal musical construction. In *Peter and the Wolf,* it is clear that Prokofiev's management of the musical material goes beyond compositional technique as each listener will hear and respond to something uniquely personal in this masterpiece. An important function of this (and other music) is the presence of a sonic pathway that provides an aural entry into listeners' own fantasies and unconscious processes.

As we take leave of Prokofiev's musical zoo, we note that Peter, the music, and all the animals have shown us that musical and psychoanalytic concepts can be used to enhance each other. When heard for the last time in *Peter and the Wolf,* the duck's theme is played by the oboe, her original signature instrument. Her theme has not been altered musically, reminding us that the animals in the mental zoo, with all their strengths and frailties, are ever-present within the human mind.

Chapter 4

Case-ette 3

Separation, Loss, Grief, and Growth – Mozart in 1778, Piano Sonata in A Minor, K. 310

> Dearest Papa! I cannot write in verse, for I am no poet. I cannot arrange the parts of speech with such art as to produce effects of light and shade, for I am no painter. Even by signs and gestures I cannot express my thoughts and feelings, for I am no dancer. But I can do so by means of sounds, for I am a musician."
>
> (Wolfgang Amadeus Mozart, November 8, 1777)

In the summer of 1778, at the age of twenty-two, Mozart composed his A Minor Piano Sonata, one of only two times he used this tonality for a full composition. Marked by its sense of gravity and its departure from both his own and others' compositional styles, this work draws attention to the distinctive yet elusive representation of affect through the nonverbal medium of music. Music without a narrative is emphasized in this case-ette, in contrast to the previous case-ettes that discussed Prokofieff's programmatic music *Peter and the Wolf,* and the song "Gee, Officer Krupke" from *West Side Story*, which had lyrics. Music without stories or lyrics invites further reflection on the affinities between music and the words spoken in psychoanalysis.

Noy has conceptualized the relationships among tone, nuance, and inflection in ordinary speaking as the "music of speech" (1993, p. 135). Paradoxically, it is this music of speech that enables us to communicate about the language of music. Beginning with a discussion of the events that gave rise to the composition of the A Minor Sonata K. 310, I will examine Mozart's musical language to illustrate how the formal properties of music intersect with certain central psychoanalytic concepts.

Mozart in 1778

Mozart's biographers usually emphasize his relationship with his father, Leopold. My focus here centers upon the psychological impact of the untimely death of Mozart's mother, Anna Maria Pertl Mozart, in July 1778, in Paris, and his musical compositions during that fateful summer. At his father's behest and accompanied by his mother, Mozart had traveled to Paris that year to seek fame and fortune. This was the first time he and Anna Maria had traveled together without Leopold.

Mozart's playful and romantic relationship with his cousin, Maria Anna Thekla – affectionately known as the *Basle* ("little cousin") – is well known and preceded his 1778 trip to Paris. The "Basle letters" (written in late 1777 and 1778) exchanged between them are laden with obscenities, private jokes, word play, riddles, excremental and sexual innuendoes, and puns. In an earthy letter to his mother (and perhaps rivaling any that he exchanged with his cousin), while anticipating their travels together, Mozart penned the following rhyming message:

Oh, mother mine!
Butter is fine.
Praise and thanks be to Him
We're alive and full of vim.
Through the world we dash,
Though we're rather short of cash.
But we don't find this provoking
And none of us are choking.
Besides, to people I'm tied
Who carry their muck inside
And let it out, if they are able,
Both before and after table.
At night of farts there is no lack,
Which are let off, forsooth, with a powerful crack.
The king of farts came yesterday
Whose farts smelt sweeter than the May.
His voice, however, was no treat
And he himself was in a heat.
Well, now we've been over a week away
And we've been shitting every day.
Wendling, no doubt, is in a rage
That I haven't composed a single page:
But when I cross the Rhine once more,
I'll surely dash home through the door
And, lest he call me mean and petty,
I'll finish off his four quartetti.
The concerto for Paris I'll keep, 'tis more fitting.
I'll scribble it there some day when I'm shitting.
Indeed I swear 'twould be far better fun
With the Webers around the world to run
Than to go with those bores, you know whom I mean,
When I think of their faces, I get the spleen.

But I suppose it must be and off we shall toddle,
Though Weber's arse I prefer to Ramm's noddle.
A slice of Weber's arse is a thing
I'd rather have than Monsieur Wendling.
With our shitting God we cannot hurt
And least of all if we bite the dirt.
We are honest birds, all of a feather,
We have summa summarum eight eyes together,
Not counting those on which we sit.
But now I really must rest a bit
From rhyming. Yet this I must add,
That on Monday I'll have the honor, egad,
To embrace you and kiss yours hands so fair.
But first in my pants I'll shit, I swear.

Adieu Mamma

Worms, January 31   Your faithful child
Anno 1778.   With distemper wild.
                                                  TRAZOM
        (Anderson, 1938, Vol. 2, pp. 673–5; 1966, Vol. 1, pp. 456–7)

The poem indicates Mozart's lack of enthusiasm about the impending trip, while vividly illustrating the playful way in which he communicated with his mother. While such language and discourse were common in Mozart's time, Mozart was perhaps more creative than others in his use of colorful vocabulary.

Letters to her husband indicated that Anna Maria Mozart consented to the journey and remained on the trip despite her increasing poor health:

> I am busy packing and this gives me a great deal of trouble, for I am doing it all by myself, since Wolfgang cannot help me the least little bit .... My fingers are aching horribly ... and I am sweating so that the water is pouring down my face .... The devil take all traveling.
>
>   (Anderson, 1938, Vol. 1, p. 450; 1966, Vol. 1, p.307)

Anna Maria's reason for accompanying her son was ostensibly to keep him from straying socially and sexually:

> When Wolfgang makes new acquaintances, he immediately wants to give his life and property .... We must not lost sight of our own interests .... In short, he prefers other people to me .... I do not consider his journey to Paris with Wendling at all advisable. I would rather accompany him myself .... I am writing this quite secretly, while he is at dinner.
>
>   (Anderson, 1938, Vol. 2, pp. 683–4; 1966, Vol. 1, p.463)

Although Mozart's professional prospects in Paris were hopeful, they were not realized. The losses he experienced with love objects (the *Basle* and later Aloysia Weber) were paralleled by a loss in musical productivity. From his arrival on March 23, 1778, until his return to Salzburg in January 1779, Mozart composed little. He hated the Parisian nobility and found his proposed patron, Friedrich Melchoir Grimm, the embodiment of Friedrich's last name.

Dismayed at vocal music performances he heard in Paris, Mozart wrote to his father on April 5, 1778:

> Let me never hear a French-woman singing Italian arias. I can forgive her if she screeches out her French trash, but not if she ruins good music! It is simply unbearable.
> (Anderson, 1938, Vol. 2, p. 770; 1966, Vol. 2, p. 522)

On May 1, his disillusionment growing, he wrote to his father:

> As far as music is concerned, I am surrounded by mere brute beasts .... must not think I exaggerate when I talk thus of the music here. I must endure it for your sake .... I shall hack my way through here as best I can, and I hope to get out without any bones broken.
> (Anderson, 1938, Vol. 2, pp. 787–8; 1966, Vol. 2, p. 533)

Another letter from son to father on May 29 suggests that Mozart was depressed:

> I often wonder whether life is worth living. I am neither hot nor cold – and don't find much pleasure in anything.
> (Anderson, 1938, Vol. 2, p. 804; 1966, Vol. 2, p. 544)

It was not long after their arrival that Anna Maria wrote home that:

> Our capital has become very small .... As for my own life, it is not at all a pleasant one. I sit alone in our room the whole day long as if I were in gaol.
> (Anderson, 1938, Vol. 2, pp. 766–7; 1966, Vol. 2, pp. 519–20)

Funds dwindled, commissions did not materialize, and by May 1, Anna Maria began complaining to her husband about developing illnesses, writing that:

> [For] About three weeks, I have been plagued with toothache, sore throat, and earache .... The rooms are cold even when a fire is burning. If by any chance Count Wolfegg is coming to Paris and could bring me a black powder and a digestive one, I should be very glad.
> (Anderson, 1938, Vol. 2, p. 788; 1966, Vol. 2, p. 534)

Leopold was unsympathetic toward his son, and apparently did not show his wife much empathy either. In a letter written May 6, Leopold advised his wife:

> Do not forget to be bled.
> (Anderson, 1938, Vol. 2, p. 792; 1966, Vol. 2, p.536)

Anna Maria Mozart died in Paris on July 3, 1778, at age fifty-seven, having almost expired twenty-two years previously while giving birth to Wolfgang, preceded in death by five of her other children.

On July 3, 1778, Mozart delayed writing to his father, and instead wrote the following to his friend Abbe Bullinger in Salzburg:

> Mourn with me, my friend! This has been the saddest day of my life – I am writing this at two o'clock in the morning. I have to tell you that my mother, my dear mother, is no more! God has called her to Himself .... I beg you, most beloved friend, watch over my father for me and try to give him courage .... I commend my sister to you also with all my heart. Go to them both at once ... but do not tell them yet that she is dead ... just prepare them for it. Use every means to comfort them ... but so act that my mind may be relieved ... and that I may not have to dread another blow.
> (Anderson, 1938, Vol. 2, pp. 828–30; 1966, Vol. 2, pp. 559–60)

With goodwill rather than truthfulness, he wrote to his father on the same date to say that his mother was "very ill" (Anderson, 1938, Vol. 2, pp. 823–4; 1966, Vol. 2, p. 556), and six days later wrote again to inform Leopold and his sister of his mother's death:

> When I wrote to you, she was already enjoying the blessings of Heaven – for all was then over. For as I judged from my own grief and sorrow what yours would be, I could not indeed bring myself suddenly to shock you with this dreadful news.
> (Anderson, 1938, Vol. 2, p. 830/1966, Vol. 2, p. 561)

On July 31, 1778, he sent more details:

> I had never seen anyone die .... How cruel that my first experience should be the death of my mother. I dreaded that moment most of all .... I had to leave her in the hands of the doctor. I went about it as if I was bereft of my reason. I had ample leisure for composing, but I could not have written a single note.
> (Anderson, 1938, Vol. 2, pp. 865, 867; 1966, Vol. 2, p. 583, 585)

In writing to Wolfgang after having received the tragic news, Leopold accused his son of matricide:

You had your engagements, you were away all day .... Her illness became more serious, in fact mortal – and only then was a doctor called in, when of course it was too late .... Divine Providence preserved your mother's life when you were born, though indeed she was in very great danger .... But she was fated to sacrifice herself for her son in a different way.

(Anderson, 1938, Vol. 2, p. 876; 1966, Vol. 2, p. 590, 591)

Anna Maria Mozart's death and her burial in Paris were followed by the news that Aloysia, Mozart's primary love object after his cousin, Maria Anna Thekla (the "little *Basle*"), had become engaged to a singer in Munich. In September 1778, Mozart reluctantly, but in obedience to his father's demands, left Paris for Salzburg. Thus, in a short time span, he lost three women who were very close to him: his mother, his cousin, and Aloysia Weber. Efforts to move away from Salzburg were dashed once he returned to his home there; he was professionally unsuccessful, musically unproductive, grief-stricken, and motherless.

Refuting his father's accusations proved futile, and the Paris trip culminated in the estrangement of father and son. There was also a permanent rupture with the Archbishop of Salzburg, increasingly separating Mozart from the domination of fatherly figures. Further, his relationship with the Catholic Church loosened; eventually, he embraced Freemasonry. His continual mismanagement of money only increased the frosty climate between son and father.

According to Einstein (1945), from the composer's Paris period we have several choruses, ensembles, and arias, various assorted pieces (which have been lost), a *sinfonia concertante* (also lost), some ballet music, and a couple of symphonies. Mozart was not compensated for his commissions in Paris, and any hope of succeeding there had rapidly dwindled. He wrote about this to his father on July 31, 1778:

He [i.e., Duc le Guines] has already had, for the last four months, a concerto of mine for flute and harp – K. 299 – for which he has not paid me .... These stupid Frenchmen seem to think I am still seven years old, because that was my age when they first saw me .... They treat me here as a beginner ... except of course, the real musicians who think differently. But it is the majority that counts.

(Anderson, 1938, Vol. 2, pp. 870–1; 1966, Vol. 2, p. 587)

However, two compositions dated simply "summer of 1778" – the A Minor Piano Sonata, K. 310, and the E Minor Sonata for Klavier and Violin, K. 304 – demand a closer look because they depart from Mozart's compositional norm. While some musicologists debate whether these striking compositions were written before or after the death of Anna Maria Mozart, it is undeniable that they were composed in an atmosphere of geographical and emotional upheaval during this momentous summer.

These two compositions are significant in their key choice and in their departure from Mozart's customary compositional style. For one thing, Mozart did not routinely compose in minor keys. Even more striking is the fact that the A Minor Piano Sonata (K. 310) is the only piano sonata Mozart wrote (of nineteen) in this particular key. The only other full composition by Mozart in this key is the A Minor Rondo (K. 511), for piano, composed in 1787 (the year of Leopold's death, which also saw the composition of *Don Giovanni*). Furthermore, the E Minor Sonata (K. 304) for klavier and violin is the only composition Mozart wrote in E minor.

Mozart and his musical style separate from the past

As Mozart separated psychologically and geographically from his home and family, Europe was going through a period of wars of independence – as were the American colonies. Stylistic changes were also occurring in music, creating a break with the past, similar in some ways to what happened about one hundred and twenty years later in *fin de siècle* Vienna, another period in which musical and psychological innovations were ushered in. For example, in mid- to late eighteenth-century Europe, while composers continued to write fugues and counterpoint, J. S. Bach had come to be "what might be called a posthumous musician" (Einstein, 1945, p. 144); that is, the new *galant*, or homophonic, style now made strict counterpoint seem old-fashioned.

Leopold had thoroughly educated young Wolfgang in contrapuntal composing. Yet Wolfgang failed his examination in writing "*in istile osservato*" ("in strictest style," Einstein, 1945, p. 147) when he applied for admission to the famous Academia Filarmonica of Bologna in October 1770. It was only with help and perhaps some outside persuasion that he finally gained admission to this prestigious Academia.

In 1775, Mozart wrote a contrapuntal motet that he sent to Padre Martini, his former teacher of counterpoint. Martini's response was that Mozart had written "modern" music, while Mozart believed he had created "authentic" music in the old style. It appears that this contrast between the *galant* and the "learned" styles in music – a "crisis of creative activity" (Einstein, 1945, p. 153) – paralleled Mozart's intrapsychic drama of 1778, which included an oscillation between present and past, Salzburg and Paris, old relationships and new ones, attachment and separation, and, ultimately, between life and death. Metaphorically, Mozart's fugal writing began to represent the old embedded within the new (as well as the new anchored in the old), as he developed his unique musical language and compositional style.

Mozart's Paris letters during 1778 but prior to his composing K. 310 provide clues about his complex feelings. In writing to his father on March 24, 1778, the day after his arrival in Paris, promising to "make good" (Anderson, 1938, Vol. 2, p. 764; 1966, Vol. 2, p. 518), he beseeches his father:

> I have one request to make, which is, to show in your letters a cheerful spirit.
>
> (Anderson, Vol. 2, 1938, p. 764; 1966, Vol. 2, p. 518)

In his reply to this letter, Leopold comments on his son's request

> I have enough debts already and don't know how I am going to pay them .... You would like me to be very cheerful in my letters. My dear Wolfgang! You know that honour is dearer to me than life itself. Consider the whole course of events. Remember that although I hope with your help to get out of debt, so far I have only sunk deeper and deeper. As you know, my credit with everyone here stands high, but the moment I lose it, my honour will vanish too. My good spirits depend, my dear son, on your circumstances, which indeed can restore me to health, as far as health is possible at my age. Yet I feel that your active endeavours and your anxiety to drag me out of this miserable situation are really bringing me back health and strength. Once you have made your father's happiness your first consideration, he will continue to think of your welfare and happiness and to stand by you as a loyal friend. I trust that you are doing so; and this trust revives me and makes me happy and cheerful.
>
> (Anderson, 1938, Vol. 2, pp. 772–4; 1966, Vol. 2, pp. 523–5)

Later on, five months after Anna Maria's death but prior to Wolfgang's return to Salzburg, Leopold writes to his son on December 28, 1778, revealing hostility mixed with panic:

> I have told you repeatedly that our interests and my prospects demand that you should return to Salzburg .... I am heartily sick of composing these long letters and ... have almost written myself blind .... If you had traveled straight to Salzburg ... I could have paid off one hundred gulden of our debts .... Your conduct is disgraceful .... Good God! How often have you made a liar of me.
>
> (Anderson, 1938, Vol. 2, p. 957–8; 1966, Vol. 2, pp. 644–5)

The variance in compositional style and key choices in the A Minor and E Minor Sonatas raises questions about the expression of Mozart's affects through sound, cheerful and otherwise, during the summer of 1778.

Choice of keys and tonality

Composers express themselves not only with stylistic conventions or inventions, such as contrapuntal and homophonic notation and form, but also with choices of tonality. Unlike composers of earlier periods in history, Mozart was not particularly restricted to narrow limits with instrumentation and orchestration. Johann Sebastian Bach had expanded the tonal possibilities of the keyboard with his "Well-Tempered Clavier," and instruments other than the keyboard had broader ranges in which to play. In fact, Mozart transcribed a series of fugues from the "Well-Tempered Clavier" for string trio and string quartet in keys simpler than those originally written by Bach. Yet, despite a wide choice of keys with which to express himself, Mozart used a rather narrow range of tonal vocabulary, and, as Einstein notes in regard to the opera *Don Giovanni*:

> An astonishingly narrow choice of tonalities suffices for an opera that explores the extreme limits of emotion and the deepest recesses of the soul. On the flat side, *Don Giovanni* does not go beyond E flat .... On the brighter side, A major is touched only twice, and E major only once, in the graveyard scene. We may really take D major or D minor as the main key of *Don Giovanni,* surrounded only by its most closely related keys .... Greater expression could not be attained, or with smaller means.
>
> (1945, pp. 157–8)

Between November 1777 and the end of the infamous summer of 1778, Mozart wrote seven clavier sonatas, five of them in Paris. As noted earlier, the A Minor Piano Sonata (K. 310) and the Sonata in E Minor (K. 304) for klavier and violin are particularly significant in their key choices as well as in other compositional techniques.2

According to Einstein (1945), A minor was for Mozart "the key of despair" (p. 244). We know that the remaining four Paris piano sonatas (K. 330 in C major, K. 331 in A major, K. 332 in F major, and K. 333 in B flat major) have a different dramatic impact upon the listener than does the A Minor Piano Sonata. When the latter was first performed in Paris in 1782, it was met with silence and without comment from the public.

A Minor, Mozart, and affects: mind to music or vice versa?

Cognizant of the dangers of applying subjective meanings to music – and of attempting wild psychoanalysis – I will offer brief comments about some particular, unique musical features of K. 310 as quasi-clinical data. At first glance, the A Minor Sonata seems to follow a textbook format: there is a sonata allegro first movement, a contrasting second movement in sonata form, and a rondo third movement. But if there is tradition in its formal, classically balanced structure, certain compositional elements nevertheless suggest that Mozart is leaving tried and true musical vocabulary behind.

For example, the tempo marking at the opening, *"allegro maestoso"* (majestically lively), is unusual; first movements in sonatas of this period are typically marked *allegro* without the *maestoso*. Further, this is the only sonata in which Mozart uses *maestoso* in a first-movement tempo marking. Thus, he verbally instructs the performer, prior to playing a note, to pace the *allegro* (or fast/quick) tempo with spaciousness, breadth, and deliberateness, modifying the usual characteristics of *allegro*.

The opening piano sounds of this piece are striking for many reasons: although a dynamic marking is not indicated at the beginning, it is customary to play it *forte* (loud). Due to the abrasive quality of the music, it has been presumed in performance practice that Mozart intended a sort of *forte* attack. The listener at once hears repetitive, unrelenting A minor chords in the left hand, over which there is a dissonant *appoggiatura* on the strong beats in the right hand (measures 1, 2, and 4).[3]

SONATE
KV 310

Figure 4.1 Beginning of Mozart's Piano Sonata in A Minor, K. 310

This is rendered even more terse by the dotted eighth- and sixteenth-note rhythm, which, in turn, produces a shocking aural (and, I believe, emotional) effect. Thereafter, melodic and harmonic dissonance as well as a percussive rhythmic persistence permeate the entire movement. These elements dominate the first thematic area – and indeed the entire sonata – as unifying devices, in varying, multiply determined permutations.

The sonata's second theme, in the relative major key of C major, continues to reflect the first theme in its repetitive material in both hands. While the left hand is more obviously insistently so, the repeated-note figure is also represented in the right-hand scale passages. Harmonically, the right hand outlines a series of falling fifths in sixteenth notes, zigzagging through its own derivative of the *ostinato* (repeated note).

Figure 4.2 K. 310, First movement, second theme

I emphasize what is occurring in the development section, where contrapuntal treatment of the previous motifs introduces ambiguity and harmonic unrest.

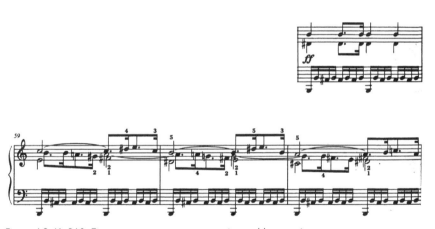

Figure 4.3 K. 310, First movement – counterpoint and harmonic unrest

Our ears yearn for resolution as this section is richly harmonic and unsettled. This section is also quite technically challenging for the pianist. In the development section, Mozart reverts to contrapuntal writing, the "learned" style of the past, while blending the tumultuous themes already presented in the exposition. This recapitulation brings back the opening material and moves toward a pianistically difficult coda. Ultimately, the movement concludes with three declamatory A minor chords, firmly resolving all dissonances, counterpoint, and rhythmic complexities (for the moment).

Figure 4.4 K. 310, first movement – conclusion

The sonata's second movement, like the first, is introduced with a verbal qualifier that modifies the andante marking: *"con espressione"* (with expression). Musically, the affect here contrasts with that of the first movement in its serene nature. Whereas the first movement had few dynamic markings, the first eight measures of the second movement are highly colored. It is as though the composer used many dynamic markings to convey musical expressivity and human emotion. The appoggiatura here is much more syntonic to the quiet, melodic mood.

Figure 4.5 K. 310, beginning of second movement

The repeated-note motif, established in the first movement but now altered in mood, clearly (re)appears in the second theme played in the right hand; it evolves into a prolonged trill under which the left hand echoes the right hand previously heard. All of this is embellished with counterpoint.

Figure 4.6 K. 310, second movement – repeated note motif evolves into trill, which is echoed in left hand

Although the thematic material is clearly connected to the first movement, it is expressive, not percussive, at the outset. These changes in the middle section point to Maynard Solomon's (1995) "*adagio/andante*" model of musical juxtapositions. Emotionally, the music that follows may also reflect the duality of Mozart's affects during 1778: both the "happiness" he sought in his letters, and the stark reality of his professional disillusionment, estrangement, and profound personal loss.

The development section, in C major, evokes the opening of the first movement, but without the dotted rhythm.

Serenity soon gives way to agitation as the key shifts to C minor and the repetitive element is now exemplified in restless, left-hand triplets.

Figure 4.7a K. 310, Measures 31–36. Second movement. Development section opens in C major).

Figure 4.7b K. 310, Measures 37, 38. Second movement. Triplets in left hand and introduction of C minor

This is followed by another variation of triplet repeated notes, which soon gather into their rhythmic impetus a series of intervals of dissonant seconds (the same jarring dissonance of the opening movement). The aural effect is that of an unending search for harmonic (and perhaps personal) resolution.

Figure 4.8 K. 310, second movement. Triplets in single notes evolve into intervals of minor seconds, which evoke the dissonance of the opening of the first movement

We are finally relieved of this agitation when the opening theme returns and draws the movement to a close in the same manner in which it opened: in a classical style, with consonance restored.

The third and final movement of the sonata is marked *presto* (very fast), which is the only time Mozart uses this tempo marking in a piano sonata. The insistent dotted-note motif of the first movement is not obvious here, but the falling thirds and other intervals, with their insistent two-note phrases, nevertheless create a relentless and breathless sense of urgency in this rondo.

Figure 4.9 K. 310, third movement, beginning. Phrasing creates a sense of breathlessness

The movement is a moto-perpetual – in continuous motion – that creates an aural and theoretical link to earlier material, since the repeated notes of the opening movement are embedded in the intervalic relationships and other thematic material of the rondo. For example, the descending two-note motif achieves a similar intensity and persistence as did the repeated-note motif. Of interest, the second theme is in C minor, rather than the traditional C major (the relative major of A minor).

Figure 4.10 K. 310, third movement – second theme begins in key of C minor rather than traditional C major

This atypically distant tonal relationship is not commonly found in compositions of this period and points to Mozart's breaks with tonal tradition. Furthermore, the keyboard style makes formidable technical demands on the performing pianist with its unusual and difficult leaps – reflecting, perhaps, inner turmoil and challenges experienced by the composer during this period of composition.

Contrapuntal material returns us to the A minor theme of the opening, which is followed by a section in A major.

Figure 4.11 K. 310, third movement – A Major section

This major key appears in the midst of A minor and C minor passages; its effect is one of heightened intensity. By now the musical motifs are clearly multiply determined and aurally affective. The very end of the composition is straightforward, with repeated notes played in octaves alternating in the two hands. The movement concludes strongly, firmly, and unambiguously with a crescendo to two A minor chords.

Figure 4.12 K. 310, ending of sonata – includes insistence of repeated note figure, which recalls the opening of the sonata

Although Solomon (1995) proposes that the A Minor Sonata represents issues of "maternal/filial fusion and separation," as well as "rupturing paternal/filial symbiosis" (p. 203), this psychoanalytic interpretation cannot be verified through the lens of clinical evidence. Yet it is undeniable that Mozart's compositions of 1778 clustered around rapid, life-changing events that presumably found expression in his nonverbal language of musical expression. As he himself described: "Even by signs and gestures I cannot express my thoughts and feelings … but I can do so by means of sounds, for I am a musician" (Anderson, 1938, Vol. 2, p. 532; 1966, Vol. 1, p. 363).

Musical evidence suggests that Mozart's affects of grief, disappointment, hostility, and guilt, and his experiences of object loss – e.g., his mother's death, his leaving home (with his mother, at his father's insistence), and estrangement from his father – all interwoven with lack of professional success in Paris, are expressed musically. These intrapsychic and interpersonal issues, I suggest, are embedded in Mozart's uncharacteristic treatment of tonality, tempo markings, rhythm, dynamic emphases, uses of counterpoint, and technical demands on the pianist in the A Minor Piano Sonata K. 310 of the summer of 1778. When thinking musically and psychoanalytically about this unique work, one becomes aware that extraordinary antecedents, both musical and developmental ones, coalesced in its composition.

Thus, the distinctive A Minor Piano Sonata K. 310 is used demonstratively here as quasi-clinical material. As such, it reflects a nonverbal form of "modified free association" (Baudry, 1984, p. 578). Reflective of numerous possible emotions experienced by Mozart in the summer of 1778, this sonata may have served as an outlet for the composer's grief, disappointment, hostility, rage, and love (toward both father and mother).

Further thoughts regarding the intersection of music and psychoanalysis

Mozart's reputation as a prankster, punster, tease, and flirt has led many to observe the perennially childlike quality in the adult composer. Solomon suggests that:

> Mozart was trapped in the dilemma of longing for the remembered ecstasies of an infantilized past even as he strove to escape from the bondage of being an eternal child. Perhaps buried deep within the fabric and structure of the A Minor Sonata are the precipitates of the struggle over these insoluble issues of fusion and individuation, obligation and autonomy, love and guilt, and exile and return.
>
> (1995, p. 203)

I differ, however, with Solomon's notion that Mozart was "longing for the remembered ecstasies of an infantilized past." It is impossible to really know the composer's longings or the nature of his childhood nostalgia. Leopold Mozart (famous in his own right as a violin teacher and author) aggressively promoted his son's career from the age of five, and then psychologically thwarted it as he perpetuated his son's childlike dependence, even as he sent him abroad at age twenty-two in 1778, when he wrote to Wolfgang: "You won a great reputation as a child – and you must continue to do so, for this always was and still is my object" (Anderson, 1938, Vol. 2, p. 782; 1966, Vol. 2, p. 529).

Unquestionably, Wolfgang had a doting parent – if also an ambitious and exploitive one – in his father, as well as a loving, devoted mother (even though Anna Maria appeared to adopt Leopold's values as her own). Leopold wrote to Wolfgang after Anna Maria's death: "You were the apple of her eye. She was immensely attached to you, she was inordinately proud of you" (Anderson, 1938, Vol. 2, p. 840; 1966, Vol. 2, p. 567).

In his analysis of "typical dreams" (e.g., "Dreams of the Death of Persons of Whom the Dreamer Is Fond"), Freud cites the Bible's Fifth Commandment, a classical Greek drama, and the work of Ibsen to illustrate the hostility inherent in father–son relations. Looking beyond the "ancient family" (1900, p. 257) and the original Greek oedipal drama, Freud writes, "Fathers are as a rule inclined to refuse their sons independence and the means necessary to secure it and thus to foster the growth of the germ of hostility which is inherent in their relation" (p. 257).

Indeed, we read in a letter written shortly after Wolfgang's arrival in Paris that Leopold was perpetuating his son's childlike dependence upon himself and, by extension, upon a transferential, patronizing figure:

> I now urge you very strongly to win, or rather to preserve *by a complete and childlike* [italics added] *trust* [italics in original] the favour, affection, and

friendship of Baron Grimm, to consult him in all matters, to act on your own judgment or preconceived ideas, and constantly to bear in mind your interest and in this way *our common interest* [italics in original].

(Anderson, 1938, Vol. 2, p. 771; 1966, Vol. 2, p. 523)

In the unrelenting promotion of his son, was Leopold's envy, like his hostility, far from the surface? Likewise, did Wolfgang's manifest obedience and wish to please conceal unconscious motives to defy and defeat his father, thus preserving childhood fantasies of triumph and omnipotence? Greenacre (1957) maintains that creative activity and aggression are linked in a manner that enables hostility to assume the role of a *positive* developmental or growth force, which results in the "capacity to turn emotional drive to artistic creation" (p. 67). Are these events and relationships the makings of childhood ecstasy?

That Mozart *could* leave his father and his home and productively survive the death of his mother is testament to his ego strength, and perhaps to a "good enough," if far from ideal, childhood. As emphasized in the foregoing musical analysis of the A Minor Piano Sonata, K. 310, he also left and/or altered the musical style and traditions of his childhood. Perhaps an adaptive dimension to Mozart's ego is seen in his fluidity in regressing to primary process in the service of his creative musical ego, while yet maintaining the capacity to combine this with compositionally productive secondary process. These qualities are also apparent in those of his letters that highlight his regression to anality and his return to genitality – the shifting back and forth between child and adult. One could hypothesize that Mozart's intrapsychic conflicts and interpersonal struggles enhanced his creative activity. Artistic growth, particularly as evidenced in the A Minor Piano Sonata, K. 310, continued unabated even when psychological development was jeopardized, suggesting a conflict-free sphere of ego functioning as well as access to libidinal and other psychic energies.

Psychological and musical complexities are verbally reflected in the letter/poem that Wolfgang wrote to his mother on the eve of their travels in 1778 (see Anderson, 1938, Vol. 2, pp. 673–5; 1966, Vol. 1, pp. 456–7). In this letter, we witness Mozart's ability to play – both with words and with his mother – and to use humor and bawdiness in a way that accesses the emotional attachments and the anality of his early years. This letter allows us to witness his wide range of affects, experiences, and surroundings, as well as his bodily awareness and his accessibility to an earlier stage of life, all of which found verbal expression in letter writing. At first glance, this letter may be shocking in its graphic use of primary process and gleeful potty talk. Despite social and cultural acceptance of descriptions of anatomical intimacies and of defecation in everyday speech in Mozart's time, Wolfgang's fascination and creative, persistent preoccupation with expressing himself in this manner are at once strikingly childlike *and* sophisticated, demonstrating his ability to access multiple psychic resources, and to move back and forth with fluency among developmental stages.

There is a similar fluency to Mozart's musical style, particularly so in his A Minor Piano Sonata, K. 310. In this case, musical notation, phrasing, rhythm, harmony, and dynamic color capture drama, intensity, playfulness, seriousness, humor, elegance, and beauty, illustrative of Mozart's wide range of affects and the fact that these were equally matched by his range of technical and musical skills (see Marshall, 1993).

Since we know that Mozart started composing at the age of five, we also know that music was an early mode of expression for him, a means of attachment, identification, preverbal and nonverbal communication, and a symbolic language. Nass (1971) discusses auditory communication and perception as a nexus of communication between mother and infant. Kohut and Levarie (1950) suggest that sounds come from external and internal sources that have – or develop through associations – affective significance. Kohut (1957) further maintains that, for the mature psyche, sonority and form allow a "catharsis for primitive impulses, and musical activity constitutes an exercise in mastery ... a form of play .... Music is an expression of rules to which one submits" (quoted in Feder *et al.*, 1990, p. 26).

Music and musical composition were likely forms of play for Mozart, providing a sense of mastery, a discharge of libidinal energy, and a means of establishing object relationships. History has created and perpetuated the myth of Mozart as the "Eternal Child." In fact, this "child" was thrust into adulthood at a tender age by his entrepreneurial father, growing up in a family in which, by virtue of his musical genius and his father's demands, he became his parents' support. Furthermore, Wolfgang lost his mother in unusual circumstances as he was leaving the bosom of his family – ironically, at his father's command. His attempts to separate and yet to maintain family ties remained a lifelong struggle.

Utilizing historical, musical, and psychoanalytic perspectives, we might conceptualize the A Minor Piano Sonata, K. 310, as a product of multiply determined factors – i.e., as a transitional object with emotional links to the past; as a channel for affective discharge of rage, guilt, and grief; and as a vehicle for mastery and movement beyond both childhood attachments and traditional musical canons. Thus the year 1778, which marked so many profound personal and musical changes for Mozart, left the legacy of the A Minor Piano Sonata, K. 310, as well as the E Minor Sonata, K. 304. Both these remarkable compositions harkened back to the Classical era in music and, perhaps, to earlier developmental periods in the composer's life. I believe they also reflected Mozart's state of mind in the summer of 1778, even as they foreshadowed the future of music in the Western world.

Mozart in the consulting room

An emphasis on the events of Mozart's life as the context for the multiply determined musical elements in the A Minor Piano Sonata, K. 310 – while simultaneously considering affects and latent meanings as they may be related to drives and their derivatives, to object relationships, and to the overdetermined functions of the ego through extraordinary nonverbal, musical pathways – provides alternative ways to think about psychoanalytic theory and practice. In adopting this broad perspective, we transcend the clinical arena and focus a spotlight on *music itself*, which is then conceptualized as quasi-clinical data. Music enhances our understanding of mental functioning and demonstrates how psychoanalytic concepts may be represented within it. A return to the consulting room further highlights the power and vicissitudes of melodies of the mind, heard by both analysand and analyst.

Ms. A had been struggling to find words to express intimate feelings toward me, her analyst, which had been evoked during a session. She associated to a memory from early childhood in which she tenderly recalled snow glistening under evening lights. This led to further associations about her love of sparkling jewelry, especially diamonds. The melody of the song "Twinkle, Twinkle Little Star" entered her mind. Her voice broke as she welled up with tears.

Her associations drifted to early childhood and a faint memory of her father, of whom she had only vague recollections, and a walk they had taken together on a snowy evening. He had mysteriously left the family shortly after this, never again to make contact. Ms. A had always wondered what caused her father to leave, and our work frequently centered upon her fantasies that she had done something to precipitate his abrupt departure and permanent silence thereafter. Through her tears, Ms. A – softly, plaintively, and longingly – began to hum and then to verbalize some well-known lyrics that had particular significance for her:

Twinkle, twinkle little star,
How I wonder where you are.
Up above the world so high, like a diamond in the sky…

As I listened and silently resonated with this familiar song, I was deeply moved by the fusion of her memory of familial togetherness and paternal longings that we could now begin to explore together. We had worked on her father's absence as a core issue, as well as on her mother's depression and her mother's dependency upon Ms. A for her own emotional support. Yet for all of Ms. A's cognitive understanding of the dynamics underlying her yearnings, her longing for love (which she felt was unrequited and frustrated in the transference), it was the *music* that first moved us to a new level of verbal discourse, one in which we could integrate old themes and eventually come to a new understanding.

Ms. A's musical memory invited me, viscerally and yet also melodically, to experience her longings in my countertransference. Not only was I able to tune into losses and unsolved mysteries in my own familial past, but also, as I listened to her music, I thought of an article on Mozart I was writing at the time. (That article was an earlier version of this chapter.) Mozart's biographical themes of familial loss, separation from his father, death of his mother at a critical maturational point, and paternal accusations of having killed her were similar to themes in Ms. A's fantasy about her father's absence, as well as her wishful fantasies that had been created to fill a void left by the unknown.

The associations that came to my mind as I thought about Mozart's summer of 1778 led me to another of his compositions: a set of variations on the children's song "Ah, vous dirais-je, Maman" (K. 265), popularly known as the "Twinkle, Twinkle Little Star Variations." When she hummed this tune, Ms. A and I connected through our respective associations to Mozart's music. Our relationship deepened, as did our understanding of her grief, guilt, unrequited love, and longings that had been with her since early childhood. The stimulus of music created fresh dynamic pathways that resulted in psychic integration for both patient and analyst as we continued our work together.

In *The Haunting Melody* (1953), Theodore Reik, an eminent psychoanalytic theoretician and writer, provides many examples of the ways in which melodies that occur to both patient and analyst during and between sessions offer clues to affect and unconscious processes. He holds that latent and manifest content, as well as transference and countertransference, are infused with musical memory: "The intangible that is invisible as well as untouchable can still be audible. It can announce its presence and effect in tunes, faintly heard inside you" (p. 12).

As illustrated by what we know of Mozart's life and by my patient Ms. A, haunting melodies in the mind, displaced from their original sources and imbued with affects and multiple determinants and meanings, have much of significance to tell us, both inside and outside the consulting room.

Chapter 5

Case-ette 4
Jealousy and Murder – Verdi's *Otello*[1]

There is much to learn in the consulting room by tuning in to the patient's musical experiences and associations and the analyst's reactions to them. My patient Ms. O enjoyed music but was not particularly musical. She did not play an instrument but at times she would refer to songs she liked, and we would analyze her associations to them. These exchanges yielded meaningful material that deepened her analysis.

Ms. O was quite articulate, concrete, and obsessive. Her affect was restricted to a small range, and her voice was typically monotone. I usually experienced her as emotionally flat and distant. Her emotional inhibitions accompanied her dread of being overpowered by her affects, many of them unknown but amophorously experienced as bodily symptoms and anxiety about performance. She had difficulty becoming engaged in relationships, which was a major focus of our work.

One day, she entered my office humming softly. A portion of our dialogue in that session follows because I believe it was music that enabled Ms. O to access, feel, express, and articulate emotions that had been previously unavailable to her. Music served to loosen her defenses as it affected her viscerally, narrowed the emotional distance between us, and provided a stimulus for further analytic work.

JJN: I notice you were humming a tune as you came in today. [*It was not usual for me to speak first, but I resonated to her music and the atypical way in which she entered my office. Even though I uttered the first words, it was Ms. O who had opened the session with the first note.*]

Ms. O: I didn't realize that. I was listening to the radio on the way here and heard some incredible music – I know how hard it's been to bring out my emotions with you, but with music I get emotional …. I feel feelings, inspiration, joy, sadness. I wish I could have shared that music on the radio.

JJN: You shared it with me as you walked in today.

Ms. O: I didn't know I was humming so loudly that you could hear. These emotions are stirred by music. I don't get stirred by many things.

What is it about music? With music I can sit in a chair, but my body can move to the beat .... It feels good. I almost always have some song in my head.

JJN: Do you now?

Ms. O: Yes, I do. [*She names a song.*] I feel empty when the room is silent. It's hard to be alone with myself. I get thoughts and music can be a distraction .... A song in my head buffers that. If I have music with me, it's more tolerable. I think my sister would have enjoyed the music I just heard on the car radio – I called my sister on my cell phone and told her that she would have enjoyed this music.

JJN: Do you think I would have, too?

Ms. O: I'm sure you would. Why am I telling you this? I want to share what I experienced and that includes with you. Usually when I come here, I share negative thoughts with you; it's unusual I want to share anything positive. This is such a difference. I can get anxious when it is silent here .... A song in my head eases my anxiety. I never thought to talk about it; I never thought to analyze it. Music is tied to memories ... like old recordings of earlier times. Why am I going back there?

JJN: You talk about music and earlier times in your life. Is music tied to what you are feeling now with me?

Ms. O: It's emotional and personal. The hard part is that I don't know how to articulate it .... It's a feeling. Music is tied to memories ... to other times in my life. It makes me get shivers down my spine. I hear sound and see and feel it, like a texture .... I can't reproduce it. The experience involves a lot of my senses. Yes, I believe you would have liked the music on the radio.

In his article "The Meanings and Functions of Tunes That Come into One's Head" (2006), Lipson concludes that "thinking in music" can be "used for expressive, defensive, and adaptive purposes" (p. 877). Lombardi (2011) explores bodily sensations as a pathway to helping individuals experience affect and use their minds in the face of strong emotion. He addresses the "complex mental relationship with the world of physical sensations and emotions" (p. 20), emphasizing an "internal musical dimension" (p. 3) waiting to be recognized.

Ms. O's "internal musical dimension," as revealed through her associations and sensations to the sounds inside her, suggests that she entered her session thinking (unconsciously) and feeling in music. Finding a verbal outlet within the context of our relationship, at first unknown to either of us, proved transformative. We both felt more connected to each other as her defenses loosened. She was able to tolerate the idea of our separateness as unique individuals, as well as our togetherness with its inherent limitations and boundaries.

In the remainder of the session just described and those that followed, affects and thoughts that had previously been unavailable emerged, particularly in relation to her feeling too humiliated to share her deepest and most embarrassing views and her fears of being overwhelmed by emotion. She came to realize that she held fast to the belief that discovering and then revealing this aspect of her inner world would lead to my disgust and abandonment of her. Furthermore, we learned that this was connected to the termination of analysis and the solace provided by music "during silences." These realizations were traced back to earlier screen memories and fantasies of being flawed, the feeling that "something is wrong with me." As we discovered during her analysis, early trauma had become displaced and represented in physical symptoms and self-defeating behaviors.

Additional memories emerged about comforting lullabies that had been hummed to Ms. O in childhood. Fantasies about and recall of her father's "volatile temper," including her identification with him, were indicative of the multiply determined meanings inherent in sounds/silences as well as words.

Ms. O and I were able to work on the idea that her internal music could be called upon adaptively during periods of stress. She became better able to use her mind to counter her previously held belief that she might become overwhelmed by emotion to the point of decompensating. The stimulus of music – the unknown and unheard melodies in her mind – opened new psychic pathways for Ms. O. Music became one of a number of overdetermined elements that served as instruments of intrapsychic change in the face of external pressures, memories, and affects. For Ms. O, tuning in to and analyzing her humming – which she could not deny emanated from inside her – allowed for greater psychic integration beyond the intellectual, rigid control she had previously and speciously depended upon for emotional safety. Attempts to avoid her own anxiety resulted in inhibition, self-denial, obsessive thought patterns, and inflexible daily routines that had held her hostage and had led to a negative self-image, with consequent rocky relationships and a stalled career.

My discussion of Ms. O's internal music modulates to my examination of the Bacio (Kiss) theme in Verdi's opera *Otello*. Music is a dynamic process of organized sounds and silences that occur in notational, harmonic, rhythmic, and temporal concert time, but is also a process that becomes – as does an analytic process – a part of one's internalized timelessness. Thus, music's sonic signifiers have the capacity to evoke latent fantasies, screen memories, and bodily sensations that in turn have the potential to link the psychic past with the present, to join affect with idea, and feeling with meaning. Isn't this what Ms. T (see Part I), Ms. A (see Mozart, Part II), and Ms. O and I discovered as we analyzed our mental melodies? Isn't this what we analysts and therapists strive for in clinical work?

In the following section, I will probe the symbols and forms of music as compared to certain underlying mental concepts that are analyzed in clinical work. Scenes from Verdi's *Otello* will be used to illustrate these interrelated ideas.

More than the notes: manifest and latent

I wrote an earlier version of this chapter shortly after September 11, 2001. At that time, I was invited by my psychoanalytic Institute to participate in an interdisciplinary program with the Michigan Opera Theater, which was staging a performance of Verdi's penultimate opera, *Otello*. As I became immersed in Verdi's music, certain scenes from the opera and my own horrified reactions to the events of that catastrophic September morning became increasingly associated with each other. I realized that Verdi's music "spoke" to me in a way that – despite the tragedy of Boito's libretto (adapted from Shakespeare's play) and the horrific events of September 11 – provided, strangely, a sense of inner comfort. This was not the comfort that one might experience when at peace within oneself, but rather a way of finding a place deep within myself where I could locate an anchor despite whatever else this unspeakable event ignited. Upon reflection, I saw that it was the inability to find words that led me to the music. What was inherent in Verdi's music that resonated in me when words felt futile and ineffective?

In my discussion of *Otello*, I will isolate Verdi's choices regarding specific harmonies in the Bacio theme to illustrate the use of certain techniques in musical language that evoke emotional responses. In doing so, I am attempting to discover why this music in particular resonated so strongly in me when I heard it around the time of September 11, 2001.

When I first experienced *Otello*, I knew nothing of its formal musical structure and yet felt profoundly moved, particularly by the Bacio melody. At first glance, the task of analyzing the nonverbal elements in this music appeared daunting. Epstein (1993) refers to a "search for the missing element" that he maintains is challenging "not least because of the intangibility of what one seeks .... Often it is the affective grasp of the music that feels insufficient .... How does one use reason ... to grasp what is fundamentally not understood via reason?" (p. 101). Clearly, searching for the intangible and the "unreasonable" is of interest to psychoanalysts. The search for elusive verbal, visual, and sensory representations in mental life is enriched by sensitivity to the musical auditory realm.

In his well-known book *What to Listen for in Music* (1957), composer Aaron Copland writes: "Whether you listen to Mozart or Duke Ellington, you can deepen your understanding of music only by being a more conscious and aware listener – not someone who is just listening, but someone who is listening *for* something" (1957, p. 19, italics in original). Listening "*for* something" includes an examination of tonality (e.g., harmony), which is one of many overdetermined musical techniques that provide sound with organizing functions. Tonality will be emphasized here to illustrate the "intangible" yet audible in *Otello*. The ways in which a composer uses tonality and harmony provide an organizing function not only to music, but to mental life as well.

When referring to selected harmonic analyses in *Otello*, I acknowledge that the isolation of harmony or of any other musical technique cannot do full justice to the multifaceted psychic compromises inherent in music for composer, listener, or writer. Nevertheless, there is an orderly process within a specific symbolic system of the musical syntax of tonality used by Verdi (representing the composer's intrapsychic complexities) that evokes conscious and unconscious emotional responses in listeners. One need not be musically trained to understand the technical implications of tonal/harmonic relationships or to experience their expressive impact.

Within five minutes of its opening, we become emotionally engaged participants in Verdi's opera. What we hear and see in the early moments of a performance of *Otello* sets the stage for what will unfold. Core issues and musically thematic material are present from the opening note, but – similar to a psychoanalytic evaluation or the opening phase of an analysis – it is not known how these acoustic clues will develop. Opening without a prelude or an overture (an unusual compositional gesture in this genre), the opera begins with a violent storm and an anxious crowd of Cypriots waiting at the dock for the return of their governor, who has been victorious in a battle against the Turks. Otello's ship weathers the storm. He enters, strong and triumphant, and sings thirteen measures – exulting in his heroic conquest. Otello then immediately leaves the stage.

Dramatically, it is quite unusual for a major character to make a grand entrance without a virtuoso aria. Musically, the fierce storm that ushers in the spectacle and the mood begins on a dissonant cluster of notes – C, C sharp, and D – in the organ pedal, notes that are heard before Otello's entrance and that continue to sound until the storm has abated, some fifty-three pages into the first act. The music, heard above the lowest note of the cluster (C), like the storm, is unsettling; it creates a sense of agitation and tension as it searches for emotional and harmonic resolution.

Only later, in retrospect, we come to realize that the tonality of C, as heard in the lowest sustained note of the storm sequence, also symbolically announces Otello's intrapsychic storm. At first, however, it is with Otello's majestic entrance that tonal certainty – the resolution of conflicted and ambiguous harmonic relationships – is achieved in the key of E major. This is the tonal center/home of his musical statement and, as we will subsequently discover, is also the tonal center for the Bacio music heard in Acts I and IV.

Musicologist David Lawton (1978) eloquently discusses the use of tonality in nineteenth-century operas, and specifically in Verdi's *Otello,* as a way to establish dramatic associations. I will illustrate my theses from a psychoanalytic-musical perspective by building upon Lawton's detailed, insightful comments and harmonic analysis, which I believe demonstrate the compatibility of musical and psychoanalytic analyses (with the realization that tonality is more complex than my discussion allows here).

The tonal centers of C and E are Verdi's musical techniques in *Otello* – a musical pathway that conveys an affective aural message. The use of the tonalities C and E in the Bacio music are conceptualized here as Verdi's musical and psychological compromises made from multiple conscious and unconscious possibilities available to him, even though his conscious choices had to be bound by the formal rules and requirements of music theory of the time. It is not necessary for the listener to know about tonal relationships and key choices to resonate to the way Verdi uses them in this opera. My intention here is to illustrate how tonality "works" to make *Otello* aurally and technically cohesive, powerful, and expressive.

In this example, I emphasize the tonal centers of C and E as psychic representations expressed in sound. While the import of verbal elements in opera must also must be considered in any analysis, specific elements of *music itself* will be explored as psychoanalytic data to illustrate two-way intersection points between music and psychoanalysis. My objective is to involve the reader/listener in a process of raising – or deepening – levels of awareness about "what to listen *for*" in music, as emphasized by Aaron Copland.

The Bacio theme

The Bacio theme first appears in Otello and Desdemona's love duet at the end of Act I, and reappears at the conclusion of the last act, which culminates in Desdemona's murder by Otello and Otello's suicide. Referring to the Bacio theme, musicologist Joseph Kerman (1968) maintains that "It is a famous dramatic stroke; many listeners … would have to search hard in their memory of Verdi's operas or of anyone else's to match its extraordinary feeling of summation, poignancy, and catharsis" (p. 495.) This melody, like the opening storm scene, is introduced by the orchestra rather than by the singers; thus the music is initially heard without words. Eventually, the Bacio melody is punctuated by Otello's words "*un bacio,*" sung on three notes. His phrase "*ancora un bacio*" joins the melodic line only for the last six notes on the third occasion that the melody occurs. It concludes in E major, the tonality of Otello's entrance at the opening of the opera.

Verdi's use of the Bacio theme as a "reminiscence" – i.e., as music in Act IV that evokes musical and emotional memory from Act I – deepens the dynamic interpersonal and intrapsychic transformations of the characters and, I believe, intensifies our affective responses. The two bedroom scenes – the first tender and erotic (Act I), the second delirious and murderous (Act IV) – are unified by musical ideas in which tonality choices, melody, and orchestration *foretell* (in Act I) and *recall* (in Act IV) Otello's stormy struggle within himself and with Desdemona, ultimately uniting them in death.[2]

From the musical notes that announce the opening storm and throughout the opera, Verdi tonally conveys Otello's passion, desperation, and breakdown of defenses, as well as the crumbling of his psychic structure and the dissolution of his object relatedness, all heightened by the musical search for tonal resolution. As listeners we are caught up in the musically transformative experience, as we *hear* a kiss of love become a kiss of death. The Bacio music itself symbolizes the core conflict of the opera.

Figure 5.1 The Bacio theme in Verdi's *Otello*

Conflict represented in sound

Tonal centers established early in the opera acquire overdetermined and latent meanings that permit aural clues to the characters' dynamics.[3] C is a key that foretells tragedy for Otello from the outset. The tonal area of C also musically identifies Iago's character. When Iago tells Rodrigo how he hates Otello, his music is heard in the key of C (Act I, Ricordi, p. 58; Schirmer, p. 354). Iago's version of the fight between Cassio and Montano opens in C (Act I, Ricordi, p. 139; Schirmer, p. 90). When Otello fires Cassio, premonitions of Otello's progressive breakdown begin in C major and move through C minor (Act I, Ricordi, p. 141; Schirmer, p. 92).

Lawton (1978) maintains that "Iago intends to lead Otello to C major in order to 'drag him to ruin'" (p. 215). For example, Iago sings to Otello predominantly in the key of C when he describes Desdemona's lost handkerchief as proof of her unfaithfulness, whispering his maliciously constructed account of Cassio's dream (Act II, Ricordi, pp. 272–7; Schirmer, pp. 186–91). It is in C that Otello overhears Iago and Cassio whispering, sees Cassio holding Desdemona's handkerchief, and plans to strangle her (Act III, Ricordi, pp. 378–89; Schirmer, pp. 245–57). At the conclusion of Act III, Otello decompensates in the presence of the Venetian ambassadors; this act ends in the key of C (Ricordi, p. 463; Schirmer, p. 323).

Verdi repeatedly uses the key of C to aurally associate Otello with Iago as escalating tragedy mounts for Otello. These musical gestures evoke powerful affect in the listener, who may or may not be aware of tonality or how Verdi uses the keys of C and E (as mentioned, the latter key, E, was heard as Otello's opening tonal center, announcing his arrival). During Verdi's musical working through of the opera, Otello's nobility and majesty, at first heard in the key of E, become destabilized through Iago's malevolent schemes and increasing associations with the tonal center C. Yet to speak of Otello's deception by Iago as the opera's only theme emphasized through the use of the key of C overlooks Otello's own internal precarious psychic conflicts. To highlight these conflicts from a sonic perspective, we *hear*, through C and E tonalities, a sonic version of Otello's conflict and torment.

Recall the key of E, announcing Otello's safe and much-heralded arrival at the opening of the opera, as well as the resolution of the storm. This key returns in the Bacio music at the end of Act I and again at the opera's devastating conclusion. At the close of Act I, after quelling the riot that Iago has manipulated, Otello and Desdemona tenderly reminisce about falling in love, and kiss before returning to their bed. Ominously, preceding the Bacio music in the first act, Otello's expression of love is tinged with his fear that "In darkness lies enshrouded what the Lord will bestow upon Otello" (translation by Walter Ducloux, Schirmer, p. 104). He sings in a key that, according to traditional rules of nineteenth-century harmony, should modulate to E. It does not. This creates musical and psychic tension.

Affectively compelling and compositionally brilliant, Desdemona's musical reply follows the expression of his misgivings and includes a statement of her love. She recalls her marriage vows in C major, the key associated with Iago. The music then modulates to the key of E and the Bacio music. However, this tonality does not conclude Act I; instead, the E major statement of the Bacio melody modulates to a "foreign" key, D flat major, to end Act I.

The powerful aural and psychological effect draws strength from the fact that E major has not yet permanently been established as a final tonal or psychological resolution. Only in retrospect, after Otello murders Desdemona at the conclusion of Act IV, do we realize that the original tonal statement of Otello's victorious and stormy arrival in Act I, which cadences in E (but with the ominous note C, retrospectively predictive, in the organ pedal), tonally portends that his greatness is unstable. Verdi has cleverly planted this sonic and psychic duality in our ears and minds.

When the Bacio melody reappears at the conclusion of the tragic final act, it "resolves" Otello's intrapsychic dilemma and the tonal ambiguities in the music, compellingly uniting music with words and affect with idea. Unlike the end of Act I, which modulates to D flat after the E major Bacio theme, the Bacio melody in Act IV definitively ends the opera in E major. Both Otello's greatness and his downfall are now represented in the same key.

Coda: the aural road

Verdi's musical vocabulary in *Otello* speaks to complex human narratives and emphasizes the dynamic nature of the human mind. As listeners, we may experience any number of associations and reactions, both consciously and unconsciously, including, perhaps, fright and disbelief at the ego's potential to become derailed by primal urges. Quite simply, we wish we could say, "Not me." The elements highlighted here – tonality being but one of the overdetermined musical carriers of meaning – evoke affects through aural channels. Music "works" because it has the capacity to put us in touch with the vulnerabilities, strengths, and complexities of our own psyches, allowing for regression to primal instincts while also permitting ego mastery. Music resonates uniquely with each listener's inner life.

If the verbal analysis of dreams paves an oral royal road to the unconscious, then music provides an aural road to the same destination. Music has the potential to change the performer, the listener, and perhaps the music itself, in that it can create and/or re-create perspectives and affects formerly not accessible to consciousness. We have seen how the analysis of the meaning of a tune in her head facilitated the loosening of my patient Ms. O's defenses, as did exploring Ms. A's resonance to the melody of "Twinkle, Twinkle Little Star."

Through the aural pathway of music, new meanings and adaptive solutions are discovered in old stories. In contemplating my reactions to the juxtaposition of *Otello* and 9/11, I came to understand that I had been viscerally brought in touch with an admixture of emotions that were steeped in experiences from my youngest years. These experiences involved the loss and collapse of significant relationships. My affects and memories were reignited by the collapse of the Twin Towers in New York City. It consoled me to realize that, during my earliest years, music had provided comfort and emotional connection, a function it was continuing to offer on that ominous sunny morning, and that it continues to provide now. I simultaneously take stock and ownership of the depth and complexity of my aggressive feelings that, while not expressed violently through action, are also a part of my affective repertoire. These affects, too, were evoked by the juxtaposition of 9/11 and *Otello.*

Verdi's use of tonality, specifically in the Bacio theme, leaves me simultaneously remembering, feeling reassured, and grieving. Music can do that. What I am emphasizing here, as well as in previous and subsequent chapters, is that musical sensitivities are alive in and beyond the consulting room, the concert hall, and the opera house. Verdi's Bacio theme allows us to examine the nonverbal essence of music in a composition of great sophistication, enhancing our appreciation of musical concepts, just as our appreciation of the music is enhanced by psychoanalytic concepts.

Chapter 6

Case-ette 5

Shame and Rage – The Breakdown of Lucia in *Lucia di Lammermoor*[1]

'Twas my hope that death would hide me from a doom of shame and anguish. Comfort is denied me. In despair I must languish. None will counsel me, none will aid me. Heaven and earth have both betrayed me.

(Lucia in *Lucia di Lammermoor*)

Euripides' literary insights [in *Medea*] point the way to clinical hypotheses that may guide our thinking in situations in which unbearable shame, with no apparent possibility of external or internal resolution or repair, drives a hardened vengefulness.

(Lansky, 2005, p. 462)

Gaetano Donizetti's opera *Lucia di Lammermoor* premiered on September 26, 1835, at the Teatro Fondo in Naples, Italy, and was first performed in the United States in New Orleans in 1842. In it Lucia murders her bridegroom in their wedding chamber on the night of their marriage. She succumbs to madness and dies of a broken heart. Emotionally depleted of internal and external resources, she has been betrayed and coerced (one could say seduced) by her brother, Enrico, into marrying Arturo, a nobleman, who, in exchange for Lucia, will secure her brother's financial and political fortunes in Ravenswood.

Enrico: The nuptial hour approaches.
Lucia: Ah! No, 'tis the hour of my doom approaches.
Enrico: Spare me thy vain reproaches.
           Listen to what I tell thee:
           Since William lives no more
           Our party is fallen
           Upon the throne of Scotland now will reign the hated Mary
           In this sad hour none can from ruin save me but Arturo.
Lucia: And I am the victim?
Enrico: Yes, Thou must save me.

(pp. 73–5[2])

This union will consummate Enrico's vengeance against his enemy, Edgardo, who is Lucia's forbidden lover. Meanwhile, Edgardo has sworn revenge against Enrico for killing his father and usurping his estate. Murder, madness, and suicide follow Lucia's arranged marriage.

This drama, which librettist Salvatore Cammarano modeled on a story from Sir Walter Scott's 1819 novel *The Bride of Lammermoor* (which in turn was based on a real event that took place in Scotland in 1669), is compelling and gripping. Donizetti's musical treatment of the narrative stimulates the listener's mental processes and illustrates various psychoanalytic concepts. An analysis of psychoanalytic ideas and of Donizetti's music as it pertains to Lucia's breakdown serves as quasi-clinical material.

Lucia's shame as motive for revenge

The dynamics that underlie self-regulation and self-esteem are pertinent for all the characters in *Lucia di Lammermoor* (in Lansky and Morrison, 1997b; Lansky, 1992, 2005, 2007a, 2007b, 2007c; Morrison, 1989; Lewis, 1971). Lucia's experience of her domineering mother, to be described subsequently, contributed to her preoedipal traumas, resulting in narcissistic humiliation, hatred, and rage. Her choice of a forbidden lover unconsciously fueled her real or perceived oedipal transgression and need for punishment.

Morrison and Stolorow (Lansky and Morrison, 1997b) conceptualize the complexities inherent in shame, narcissism, and underlying motives for revenge along a broad continuum of the "subjective experience of selfhood" (p. 82). They suggest that the powerful dynamics that allow regression to primitive, preoedipal states "weave historical antecedents into a tapestry illustrating the relationship between shame and narcissism" (p. 65). Such conceptualizations of shame and its vicissitudes are consonant with Cooper's (2005) "narcissistic-masochistic character" (pp. 121ff) in which oedipal conflicts reveal entrenched earlier layers of preoedipal trauma. Lansky and Morrison (1997a) discuss how shame can be masked beneath the emotions of "anxiety, guilt, envy, contempt, and reaction to narcissistic injury" (p. 4). In this context, shame is conceptualized as both an affect and a defense (Lansky and Morrison, 1997b; Morrison, 1989).

Morrison explores shame in the contexts of intrapsychic mentation and social interaction. The former is exemplified by Freud's idea that shame is a "reaction formation against the wish for genital exhibitionism" (Morrison, 1989, pp. 6–7), while the latter connotes anxiety over rejection by others. The "social embeddedness" (p. 15) of shame is also experienced through internalized objects. According to Morrison, Freud's emphasis on affects, defenses, and the vicissitudes of guilt as it pertained to intrapsychic conflict and the ego ideal evolved into the structural concept of the superego, but Freud stopped short of exploring shame in his study of narcissism (see Freud, 1914).

Piers and Singer (1953) discussed a shame/guilt dialectic, maintaining that shame reflected a perceived deficit and defect of the self, while guilt was an affective or defensive response to a real or perceived superego transgression. To avoid dichotomizing these dynamics, they suggest that we think of a "shame/ guilt cycle" (cited in Morrison, 1989, p. 11) in which "guilt and shame interact and can be interchanged" (p. 11). This conceptualization attempts to reduce the tendency to cast shame and guilt defenses and affects in either/or terms, and to minimize the tendency to assert that, developmentally, guilt replaces shame. According to Wurmser (1981), "the complex affect of shame … always involves the superego" (p. 73), implying a perspective that draws on the structural theory and oedipal conflict.

While shame and its vicissitudes will be the primary focus of my exploration of Lucia's psychodynamics, we should keep in mind that an admixture of shame and guilt were ever present in her mental life.

Moving beyond the dynamic concept of intrapsychic mentation, Lansky (2007b) examines the "instigation" of violent action when unbearable forces coalesce and one feels trapped without possibility of escape. In such circumstances, he maintains, unbearable shame becomes the "*instigator* of vengeful destructive action" that has been "shaped by the influence of paranoid shame fantasies, omnipotence, and oblivion to consequences to the loved one or oneself, or the fantasized restoration of well-being that would follow vengeful action" (pp. 32–3, italics added).

Lucia's profound humiliation and hopelessness, her increasing detachment from internal and external constraints, and her dashed hopes for reparation of object ties culminate in an act of violence. Lucia's fantasized reunion with Edgardo as an oedipal object in her "Mad Scene" further suggests preoedipal and oedipal fantasies about destruction of her mother and union with her father.

Lucia's downward spiral and psychic disorganization precede the action of *Lucia di Lammermoor*. Devalued (offstage) by her mother in Scott's novel, betrayed by her brother in the opera (which is perhaps also suggestive of incestuous desire, though this is not overtly developed), and betrayed by her trusted confidant/cleric, Raimondo – as well as geographically and emotionally abandoned by her lover, Edgardo (who leaves for France and who has been quick to doubt her faithfulness) – Lucia acts. Motivated by conflicted longings for union and destruction, guilt and shame, by despair and rage, by her evil introjects, and manipulated by pathological interpersonal relationships, she suffers a complete depletion of her adaptive intrapsychic resources.

In Donizetti's portrayal through nineteenth-century musical language – i.e., in the *bel canto* operatic style[3] – it is not difficult to *hear* Lucia's defenses and compromise formations being increasingly shattered through high notes, stunning cadenzas, and other *bel canto* techniques as the listener "locates the shame behind rage … or despair" (Morrison and Stolorow, quoted in Lansky and Morrison, 1997b, p. 82).

Lucia's marriage to Arturo ultimately brings her to "irreversible disgrace" (Lansky, 2005, p. 439). Lucia increasingly becomes an emotional orphan since she is the devalued – but, ironically, also the highly valued – property of her brother.

Enrico: In this sad hour, none can from ruin save me but Arthur.
Lucia: And I am the victim?
Enrico: Yes, thou must save me.
Lucia: Oh, brother!
Enrico: Come to the nuptials.

(pp. 74–5)

Emotionally depleted and attempting to undo her forbidden strivings for Edgardo and her brother's guilt-producing entreaty to marry the man he has chosen for her, Lucia signs the marriage contract to Arturo, sealing her own punishment.

Murdering Arturo immediately after their wedding allows Lucia to psychically resolve her intrapsychic losses, longings, disappointments, intolerable rage, shame, and guilt as she incorporates the attacking wild boar, which was introduced in Act I and is identified with her malevolent mother/brother. With her selfhood continually under both internal and external assault, she fulfills her fantasy of reunion with Edgardo in the only way left to her: through hallucination and death. Consequently, Lucia maintains "double identifications with both aggressor and victim," as her "legitimate self-assertion [was] in short supply" (Cooper, 2005, p. 129). Her irreversible torment is musically consummated in her "Mad Scene," which will be discussed subsequently.

An intersection between psychoanalysis, music, and affect

Donizetti's orchestral prelude to *Lucia di Lammermoor* evokes an ominous mood before a single word is sung. The opera opens in the key of B flat minor, with a soft timpani roll evoking distant thunder. This is followed by a solemn phrase for horns, which evolves into a mournful melody by the clarinets and other woodwinds; subsequently, a dirge rhythm joins, cumulatively predictive of smoldering intrapsychic and musical storms and actions that erupt throughout the opera, finally exploding in madness, the death of Lucia, and the suicide of Edgardo.

This grave opening atmosphere is abruptly shattered as listeners are jolted by three *fortissimo* (very loud) chords played by the full orchestra. These chords musically anticipate the deafening orchestral thunderstorm and Lucia's murderous thunderbolt in Act III. Following these chords, the funeral rhythm, now quickened and modulating to the tonality of B flat major (sonically signifying a shift in mood), is played with agitation by the tympani and horns. It is in this restless tonal and rhythmic musical environment that we hear the first words of the libretto. The brief prelude has conveyed in sound Lucia's intrapsychic premonition that "the hour of my doom approaches" (p. 73).

The fountain and *il fantasma*

Shortly after the opening prelude, we meet Lucia at a fountain. We learn from a hunter, Normanno, that Edgardo has saved her from a wild boar while she was out walking, ostensibly mourning her mother's death.

> Normanno: A sword came brightly flashing, and in a moment slain was the monster.
>
> (p. 12)

Thus, early in the opera, the manifest image of the slain wild boar not only suggests the malignant revenge motives that become palpable and audible within and among all the major characters, but also permits early clues into Lucia's self-object representations: how she sees herself in relation to others and, perhaps, others in relation to her self-image – and her intrapsychic disequilibrium.

We discover that the fountain is the location of Lucia's secret trysts with her lover Edgardo, who is envied and despised by her brother Enrico.

> Enrico: Torments of hate and vengeance . . . I'll die unless I punish him [Edgardo].
>
> (p. 13)

Edgardo is a forbidden love object for Lucia. In her aria sung at the fountain, we *hear* her – a woman who has been soul murdered (Shengold, 1989) in Ravenswood – identify with the female ghost, *il fantasma*, who inhabits the fountain. Lucia is forced to incorporate her early parental empathic failures, particularly those of her malignant maternal introject. Her terror of *il fantasma* in Act I (and again in her Mad Scene in Act III) awakens and then reawakens her ambivalent attachment, as well as, perhaps, her unconscious fantasy that some aggressive thought or act of hers (perhaps meeting her forbidden lover) has killed her mother.

On one level, Lucia's premonitions about *il fantasma* lead back to her perceived oedipal transgression or fantasies; it seems that her sense of doom and punishment portend her own death. The celestial harp we hear at the fountain musically underscores Lucia's other-worldly destination. As she gazes into the fountain – her narcissistic mirror – the terror on her face also reflects preoedipal shame and its underlying defenses and affects, including humiliation and contempt. This is consonant with Morrison's (1989) view that shame is "central to narcissistic disorders ... Rage is a response to narcissistic injury" (pp. 7–8).

In Sir Walter Scott's novel, Lucia's mother, Lady Ashton, has the reputation of being diabolical, hateful, ambitious, and domineering. She despises her husband and hates Edgardo's ancestors, whom she believes to be more prestigious than her own. She is disdainful of her daughter Lucia, whom she resents for not wanting to marry the man she has chosen for her. In Donizetti's and Cammarano's operatic collaboration, Lady Ashton has been "killed off" before the opera opens, although her presence is clearly felt throughout.

While Fisher (2003) surmises that Lady Ashton's absence in the libretto and score reflects an Italian tradition of portraying "loving mammas," eliminating her from the libretto does not erase the intrapsychic and intergenerational malevolence that casts a wide shadow upon her offspring. Guilt and shame are timeless in the unconscious, making the timing of Lady Ashton's death irrelevant in our understanding of Lucia's dynamics. Painful affects and human dilemmas do not vanish beneath the beauty of *bel canto* operatic style; in fact, they are intensified by these musical techniques. It is clear that Lady and Lord Ashton are intrapsychically as alive as the ghost that inhabits the fountain and their daughter's mental life. In displacement and in reversal, Lucia sings in Act I both about her mother and her own reflection in the fountain:

> Lucia: 'Tis the fountain,
> I tremble whenever I behold it.
> Know'st thou the legend?
> Upon this spot, they say so [musical instructions: *crescendo di forzando*]
> That a Ravenswood slew the maid that lov'd him [musical instructions: *a tempo*],
> In jealous madness
> The hapless maiden rests in its waters,
> Its tide clos'd over her for ever …
> Her wraith once stood before me
> [musical instructions: *lento* over this phrase; ascending vocal line with *crescendo*].
>
> (Act I, pp. 31–2)

Lucia's angst is heard in the music at the fountain. At the end of the first stanza of her aria, *"Regnava nel silenzio"* ("Everything was silent"), we note that Lucia's fear is heightened when the word *ecco* ("here") is sung twice, which changes the rhythm to emphasize that "here" is where the ghost (*il fantasma*) appeared to her. At this point the musical tempo changes from *larghetto* (slow) to *presto* (very fast), which, according to the conventions of *bel canto* style, denotes intensification of Lucia's affect.

Immediately following, when she sings *"l'ombra mostrarsi"* ("the ghost shows itself"), the first syllable is on the lowest note of the passage (C natural), and accents are placed above each note in the word *mostrarsi*, musically accenting the fright she experiences during her vision. (See Ashbrook, 1982, for a detailed discussion of this passage.)

Lucia's aria at the fountain enhances the musical, psychological, and dramatic forces that converge and together convey the intrapsychic, interpersonal, and intergenerational tragedy that has begun to unravel in Ravenswood.

Figure 6.1 Donizetti – Lucia di Lammermoor: Lucia's "fright" at the fountain

Irony and paradox

Several paradoxes, particularly pertinent to shame dynamics, are integral in this opera from the rise of the curtain. One is the contrast between the beauty of the music, on the one hand, and the horrific manifest and latent content and action of the story, on the other. This paradox can be explained in part by the fact that the nineteenth-century operatic techniques available to Donizetti relied on beautiful melodies, acceleration of tempi, and dazzling vocal displays to convey heightened emotion. *Bel canto* style, familiar to contemporary audiences, could be employed to convey ill-omened intrapsychic dynamics and affects.[4]

Act I immediately introduces musical and psychological irony. Lucia has responded to Edgardo's request to see her by asking him to meet her at the darkly ominous fountain, her narcissistic mirror and the wellspring of her terror. Musically, the solo harp's celestial introduction of Lucia at the fountain provides an aural statement of its symbolic importance. In addition to its intrapsychic and dramatic significance, this is a location where she is likely to be discovered by her suspicious brother. Why does Lucia unconsciously invite love, terror, and discovery in this spot?

During their meeting, Edgardo at first offers to try to make peace with his sworn enemy Enrico:

Edgardo: Ere my departure, I'll seek thy brother. There shall be peace between us, strife be forgotten, in pledge of lasting friendship, I then will ask him for thy hand.

(p. 44)

Lucia urges Edgardo to keep their relationship secret, and Edgardo explains the reason for the enmity between the two men:

Lucia: Ah, no, in silence let our love yet be hidden.

(p. 44)

Edgardo: He slew my father,
Will but my life-blood suffice him
By whose craft I am ruined?
Eternal hatred he hath sworn me
Oh vengeance!

(p. 45)

Edgardo's uncontested agreement to keep their love secret moves the story along, but casts an ominous pall on both his own and Lucia's motives, which include hardened hatred toward and envy of Enrico, who in turn despises and envies Edgardo.

This scene is manifestly problematic and musically interesting. Beneath forbidden love lurks the resolution by both Lucia and Edgardo to avenge unfinished, unforgiven business, an unconscious motive for their union. In Act II, why is Lucia so ready to believe Enrico's and Raimondo's lies about Edgardo's unfaithfulness? Why is Edgardo so quick to rage against Lucia, who, ashen and ashamed, admits to signing her marriage contract?

Furthermore, immediately after the wedding, Enrico leaves the reception for Edgardo's Castle in Ravenswood, unable to let go of his loathing even though he has ostensibly achieved his goal:

Enrico: I to death defy thee . . . . Destruction, destruction I have sworn to thee. Come, to the combat. None now shall take vengeance on thee, none but myself who have doom'd thee!

(pp. 165–6)

Lansky (2007b) observes that a person who is envied is also hated for what is admirable about him. Edgardo and Enrico hate each other and also covet what the other has, i.e. Lucia and Ravenswood, respectively – which is suggestive of their unfinished oedipal business and narcissistic rage. Lucia herself, while manifestly trying to escape her psychic heritage, bows to her brother and the memory of her dead mother in becoming Arturo's bride. At first glance, she appears to become both a victim and a disempowered woman, tangled in a web of complex jealous and hateful rivalries. It is irrefutable, however, that Lucia is herself a powerful player motivated both by revenge and her own intense hatred.

An irony of Lucia's ill-fated relationship with Edgardo is heard in the musical score. Edgardo's suicide aria in Act III is introduced in the key of D major, the concluding tonality of the opera and the parallel major of Lucia's fountain aria, "*Regnava nel silenzio,*" which progresses to D minor following its D major recitative and introductory harp prelude. The point emphasized here is that the lovers' union is never musically consummated in the same tonality.

These musical elements (and many others not detailed here) illustrate Donizetti's sensitivity to the internal lives of the characters whom he represents in sound. One does not need to be psychoanalytically or musically sophisticated to experience the potent effect of his musical techniques.

Omnipotence: another perspective on lucia's "helplessness"

On one level, Lucia's narcissistic vulnerabilities erupt in violence as a romantic-era "solution" to humiliating victimization, narcissistic rage, and forbidden oedipal fantasies. Yet murdering her bridegroom Arturo also provides Lucia with the illusion of omnipotence, and specifically of power over the dominant men around her. She identifies with male manipulation and malignance in achieving victory over the most important woman in her life, her mother. Her actions in fact represent the antithesis of victimization and helplessness.

The opera's chilling climax is reached when Lucia phallically penetrates her bridegroom with a sword ("Know'st thou the legend? Upon this spot, they say so, that a Ravenswood slew the maid that lov'd him in jealous madness" [pp. 31–2]). This gruesome act leads to the famous "Mad Scene," consummating what is in effect Lucia's triumph and powerfully uniting musical and psychoanalytic concepts. Metaphorically, in becoming the "wild boar" from whom she was saved by Edgardo in Act I, Lucia ensures that she is no longer in need of rescue by others or by her own ego; it is not necessary for her to maintain reliable object relationships. With the hindsight of Act III, the wild boar emerges as Lucia's counterpoint to her sense of victimization as a female and its companion, her terror, which were displaced onto the slain animal and *il fantasma*. Thus, the wild boar that brings the lovers together in Act I also heralds their undoing, foretelling Lucia's total destruction of Ravenswood and ultimately of herself.

Lucia's affects and actions reveal hidden complexities in her intrapsychic motivations and affects, which, like those of Enrico and Edgardo, include jealousy and a profound sense of diminishment. These are the wellspring of her inescapable shame, guilt, and self-destructiveness. In this respect, Lucia's underlying psychic structure echoes the inability on the part of the male characters to forgive past hurts and wrongdoings. Her fragile equilibrium is psychically dismantled as her resolution/solution can only be expressed through becoming "mad" enough to resort to murder, which constitutes an escalation of affect to the level of *instigation* (see Lansky, 2005). Lucia *must* kill Arturo because a marriage to him "would be tantamount to forgiveness and complicity with the world of her betrayers" (Lansky, 2005, p. 461).

Sonically, the intrapsychic and interpersonal dilemmas of Lucia, Enrico, and Edgardo gather force in *crescendos* and *accelerandos* from the opening tympani in Act I. Through every cadenza, high note, tempo change, and aria, these forces gain dramatic and emotional steam to musically portray a lethal vengefulness. Murder, for Lucia di Lammermoor, represents both psychic dissolution *and* fantasized reunion with loved and hated objects. The final heartbreak is that, ultimately, there are no winners.

Mad scene

After retiring to the bridal chamber, Lucia then re-enters the reception hall, disoriented and blood stained. She has stabbed Arturo. Her entrance is heralded by a flute (or a glass harmonica, in the autographed score), evoking an eerie and otherworldly effect with music alone (there are no words at this point). Then the flute recalls the opening of Lucia's famous love duet with Edgardo in Act I that begins "*Verrano a te*" ("They will come to you").[5] This recollection stimulates Lucia's hallucinatory fantasy of marrying Edgardo, expressed in her invitation that he come to the fountain to "let us rest together" (p. 191). In this chilling scene, the flute acts out Lucia's wordless, disoriented self/other-self, simultaneously creating an accompaniment, establishing a mood, and evoking reminiscence. The flute's melody wordlessly precedes and portends Lucia's expression of mournful confusion:

> Lucia: Oh Edgardo, why dids't thou leave me? . . . . What shudder do I feel through my veins? . . . . My heart is trembling, my senses fail . . . . Come to the fountain, there let us rest together.
>
> (pp. 190–1)

Following this passage, utilizing *bel canto*'s traditional way of conveying heightened emotion, the tempo accelerates from *allegretto* (fast) to *allegro vivace* (very fast), musically and emotionally conveying increased agitation. It is in this place in the score that Lucia begins to remember: she recalls the ghost "standing between us," the ghost that "divides us." Sonically, her memories are expressed in octave leaps and in clipped, desperate musical phrases.

Above the orchestral *tremolo*, Lucia's growing agitation and disorientation gather intensity, *accelerando*, until she becomes terrified and sings/utters, "*il fantasma, il fantasma.*" Donizetti marks this horrifying passage *forte* (loud). Harmonies become increasingly unstable, as though both Lucia and the opera's tonal structure are breaking down. The flute's recollection of her love duet unravels her. This harmonically unsettled section aurally conveys desperate and pitiful affect as we are forced to *hear* the depth of intrapsychic torment that pervades Lucia's mental processes. The music corroborates what the words articulate: the fountain's water has turned into blood; Lucia's impulses have turned into action; Lucia has become stained with the blood of murder. She *must* go mad and die; her intrapsychic anguish has been enacted.

In the final moments of her decompensation and *bel canto* vocal cadenza, Lucia can sing only in wordless syllables that portray memories of the melody of her love song in Act I.

Coda: beyond the aural road

Music, like speech, is a form of aural communication. Although the beautiful arias and vocal fireworks in *Lucia di Lammermoor* may be its most readily apparent sonic attributes – the ones most readily likened to the opera's manifest content – the music also portrays affect and latent material nonverbally. That is, it is rich and evocative both psychoanalytically and musically.

I maintain that music in general, and, specifically, the musical examples in *Lucia di Lammermoor* discussed here, activates unconscious processes and latent meanings. In this way, an opera's musical score intensifies its libretto's impact. According to Lansky (2007a), there is "something inherently different about music – different from other means of artistic expression that represent something." Citing philosopher Arthur Schopenhauer, Lansky proposes that music – in contradistinction to literature and painting (which may be more directly representational) – is a "direct conveyance of the will itself," which Lansky compares to Freud's unconscious wish.

Lansky's statement is compatible with Lipps's writing (see Lipps cited in Barale and Minazzi, 2008) about prerepresentational aspects of music, affect, and mental functioning, which – interestingly – has implications for Freud's scientific and affective detour from music (see Part I, "The Aural Road"). I agree with Lansky (2007a) that "music is a direct emissary of that emotional force, not a representation of it," and with Feder (unpublished) that music is a "simulacrum of mental life."

The music of *Lucia di Lammermoor* "works" because, more than a century and a half after it was written, it still has the power to bring us in touch with complexities in the melodies of our own mental lives. Donizetti's music deepens the artistic and affective impact of the title character's shame and guilt. Should my verbal attempt to convey her emotional and psychic structure fall short, Donizetti's music will not.

Chapter 7

Case-ette 6

Multiple (Dys)Function – Polyphony in "The Tonight Ensemble" (*West Side Story*)

Clinical prelude

Polyphony and multiple (dys)function can be illustrated clinically and musically, as will be shown in this final case-ette.

When Mr. B came to see me, he was a thirty-five-year-old student who had returned to graduate school to pursue piano studies. He had earned an undergraduate degree in music many years earlier. His overt trigger for seeking psychological treatment was his debilitating stage fright, which prevented him from performing in public with technical and mental security.

Mr. B's performance anxiety had increased since he returned to school. His symptoms included lowered concentration, a subjective perception of playing less musically, missing notes, and sweating so profusely that his fingers slipped off the keys. He was concerned about loss of motor function in his musical technique. He noted that since he had returned to school, performing had become more important to him and he had practiced harder, yet his playing had deteriorated. He observed that in the past, he could play in public with comfort and could project "great musical ideas." His goal was to perform like Arthur Rubinstein or Vladimir Horowitz.

Mr. B's story about his performing became increasingly more complex as he continued to tell me about himself and his family. Although he had earned his undergraduate degree in music, he entered the financial consulting field and joined his wealthy father's company to help repay student loans. While working in the business world, Mr. B found himself compelled to practice the piano for about six hours a day while also spending eight hours a day at the office. He said that his fatigue caused him to "screw up the customer accounts"; he almost ruined several clients' portfolios. He quickly became involved with drugs and alcohol, and, consequently, quit the family business. Subsequently, he decided to return to music school, realizing that he missed playing the piano.

Mr. B observed that his performance problems had emerged on his first day back at school. Noting that his fellow students were mostly younger, he complained, "They play like monsters, which makes me feel inferior and incompetent." Because he was older, Mr. B felt that the other students should look up to him, but the competition seemed much stiffer than before. Of note, although he had begun piano lessons at the age of six, he felt he was a late starter, pointing out that others were already playing concerts by that age. His pattern of feeling inferior and competitive was longstanding.

Developmental history

Mr. B's father left the family when Mr. B was a toddler. His mother soon remarried, causing Mr. B to experience a double rejection and to feel like an outsider. Although he reported maintaining contact with his father and being on good terms with him, he described an emotional distance between them and attributed this to his less-than-stellar achievements as a music undergraduate. His father loved music, although he did not play an instrument. Mr. B cynically described his father as a man who "plays with toys" – i.e., cars, planes, houses, women.

Mr. B reported that his stepfather often belittled him and his mother, especially when drinking, insisting that his stepson be "perfect." Mr. B did not speak about his mother in any detail. It was clear to me that that this had been a dysfunctional family, and that Mr. B's performance anxiety was embedded in multiply determined dynamics. I began to understand the underlying narcissistic issues and oedipal conflicts that accompanied him on stage, in school, and in his family. These conflicts both motivated him and inhibited him.

While a teenager, Mr. B had abused drugs and alcohol, typically after a "bad performance – when I felt unwell inside." When he was upset, he needed to be reassured that he was an okay pianist and an okay person, he said. He continued to overuse aspirin, especially before concerts, and drank alcohol when he felt lonely, which was often. A recent relationship with a woman had failed because Mr. B wanted to "have fun" while the woman wanted to "get serious." Transference implications for our work appeared in the earliest stages of his treatment with me.

Mr. B came across to me as laconic, removed, and affectively isolated from the intense experiences he reported. He commented that he was trying to keep himself from feeling any disappointment or anger. His latent, multiply determined dynamics, cloaked in the manifest symptoms of music performance anxiety, long preceded his return to graduate school. His psychological pain, which he dealt with through denial, isolation of affect, and alcohol abuse, were multiply determined and related to his rage over feeling rejected and unheard as a child, his fears of future rejection (alongside grandiose wishes for acknowledgment as a famous "virtuoso"), and his unconscious need to reject the very persons on whom he longed to depend (including his therapist).

His rage had become displaced and internalized, and he punished himself by unconsciously sabotaging his performances. Certainly, he attempted to destroy his father through nearly bringing down the family business. (Of note, performers often express a wish to "bring down the house" with appreciative and thunderous applause!) His grandiose image of himself as another Horowitz or Rubinstein, who received worldwide admiration, was incompatible with the inferior pianist (or the inferior little boy) whom he believed himself to be. Extravagant wealth and success – which he envied in his father and, by extension, in famous musicians – were not available to him through music, nor could he attain them through emulating his businessman father. His competitive spirit was thwarted by the unconscious undertow of feeling incompetent and rejected by the persons whose love he craved.

Mr. B had been forced to cope as best a child could with the sudden exit of his father from the family home when he was just two, typically an age when toddlers enjoy showing off and being the center of attention. His performance anxiety reactivated a primary fear of being abandoned by his audience (he had experienced rejection yet again in light of his mother's remarriage) when he "showed off" and competed with the "big boys" by trying to perform a virtuosic repertoire. But his inability to successfully perform both on and off stage induced affects of shame, humiliation, guilt, envy, jealousy, rage, and the wish for revenge. He felt boxed in by two unbearable options: (1) either he would be successful while young but risk rejection and loss as he gained independence and adulthood, or (2) he would fail early on and thereby remain dependent and a child. To be successful and grow up held many psychic dangers for Mr. B. Finding himself in excruciating emotional pain, he finally allowed himself to seek treatment.

At the outset of our work together, I picked up signals that Mr. B was likely to avoid closeness in our relationship at the same time that he sought it. His comments about a previous brief therapy and his lack of connection in relationships with women foreshadowed his defensive tactics with me. His ambivalence was evident from his first appointment, which he missed without calling to cancel. He was thirty minutes late for his second appointment. In the session that followed, Mr. B revealed that he felt guilty about not having phoned his mother the day before, which was Mother's Day.

Despite attempts to explore the patient's anxiety and ambivalence about coming to see me, his treatment over the first three months was punctuated by frequent absences. While he seemed relieved to conceptualize his performance anxiety as embedded in a broader context of interpersonal and intrapsychic issues, he was also threatened by the possibility of exposure of "something else even worse." His attitude toward me was a recapitulation of the thoughts and feelings he projected onto audiences: it was based on the fear that his fantasized deficits would be discovered both by those who heard him perform and by his therapist. In his mind, he had not been a "perfect" child (nor was he a perfect pianist/patient now), and he was convinced this was why people left him.

Mr. B terminated his treatment abruptly in a way that was reminiscent of the way he left both music and his father's business: he simply walked away. His dysfunctional pattern of anxiety, impulsivity, flight, and retribution continued.

My condensation of Mr. B's performance anxiety as built upon multiply determined dynamics highlights his complex intrapsychic counterpoint and interpersonal dissonant polyphony that became embedded, experienced, and enacted through manifest symptoms and enactments. How many Mr. Bs wind up as Sharks and Jets – gang members – who defensively and desperately mock, fear, and yearn for compassionate "Officer Krupkes" – parents, audiences, and therapists? How many Mr. Bs "never got the love that ev'ry child ought-a get"? (See Case-ette 1, my discussion of the song "Gee, Officer Krupke" in *West Side Story*.) How many Mr. Bs wind up with thwarted dreams, lacking morning stars that might reveal a glimmer of hope for their unheard dissonances?

Music can illustrate such complex psychodynamic pictures. A polyphony of familial, cultural, and social dysfunction and intrapsychic distress, such as that seen in Mr. B, is illustrated in the case-ette I will describe presently, about rival gang members in "The Tonight Ensemble" from *West Side Story*.

Gertrude Ticho (1967) and Pinchas Noy (2009) enhance our thinking about the polyphonic interconnection between psychoanalytic concepts and musical themes. Noy emphasizes emotion and musical polyphony. Ticho discusses the interdisciplinary values of psychoanalytic literature in the humanities, emphasizing that being moved by the work of creative artists may "broaden one's understanding of unconscious material pushing toward consciousness" (p. 314). The topic of polyphony and multiple function (or dysfunction, as the case may be) – the focus of this case-ette – whether psychoanalytic and/or musical, is a complicated one. Often during my own analysis, specific music came into my mind that evoked strong feelings, interesting associations, and yielded new insights (and, incidentally, I had the same experience in writing this book). So many thoughts would rush into my mind simultaneously that I would say to my analyst, "If only I could communicate all of this in music – because then I wouldn't be limited to speaking one word at a time."

Leaving aside the underlying dynamics of my grandiose wish to transcend the limitations of speaking one word at a time, I am in agreement with philosopher Susanne Langer (1942), who maintained that:

> The real power of music lies in the fact that it can be "true" to the life of feeling in a way that language cannot, for its significant forms have that ambivalence of content which words cannot have …. *The possibility of expressing opposites simultaneously* gives the most intricate reaches of expressiveness to music.
>
> (1942, p. 243, italics mine)

Polyphony – or simultaneously experiencing and/or expressing opposites – exists both in music and in mental life. I have attempted to emphasize and integrate these ideas in previous chapters in illustrating the psychoanalytic concepts of manifest and latent content, multiple function, overdetermination, and displacement (among others) with exemplary clinical and musical vignettes/case-ettes. In this case-ette, highlighting "The Tonight Ensemble" from *West Side Story*, polyphony and multiple function are emphasized as they are aurally integrated.

Alex Ross (2007), music critic for *The New Yorker*, maintained that "articulating the connection between music and the *outer* world remains devilishly difficult. Musical meaning is vague, mutable, and, in the end, deeply personal" (p. xiii, italics mine). I resonate with Ross and add that articulating the connection between music and an individual's inner world is equally daunting, if not infinitely more so. Daunting does not mean impossible, however.

The formal qualities of music, e.g., harmony, rhythm, melody, dynamics, tonal centers, etc., and their creative manipulations by a composer allow the listener to better integrate his or her own multiple levels of complex mental polyphony. Intrapsychic and interpersonal issues that have been unconsciously preserved are ever-ready to be reawakened by internal and external stimuli – through words, music, and/or a combination of these.

Formal properties: integration and organization – "The Tonight Ensemble" from *West Side Story*

I began my case-ettes with a discussion of musical and mental ambiguity in the song "Gee, Officer Krupke" from Leonard Bernstein's *West Side Story*. I conclude my psychomusical illustrations with another song from this masterpiece. Noy's (2009) description of a "multilevel musical message" of contrasting emotion – made in reference to Mozart's opera *Idomeneo*, "where each of four participants expresses … specific emotion at the same time" (pp. 1–2) is in my opinion equally apt for the multiple function and musical polyphony in "The Tonight Ensemble," which precedes the musical's live-action rumble, mayhem, and double murder.

In order to aurally convey the psychic and musical agendas of the Jets and their rivals the Sharks, Bernstein traverses and intermingles various tonal centers and rhythms. Each gang member individually communicates his or her own intentions, while also simultaneously singing those intentions together with the other members. In awe of the composer's genius, I wish to point out Bernstein's seamless blending of the musical and mental concepts of polyphony and multiple function. For me, "The Tonight Ensemble," which is musically and affectively rooted in the reminiscing melody of Tony's song "Tonight," rivals both the sextet in Donizetti's *Lucia di Lammermoor* and the quartet in Verdi's *Rigoletto* in its integration of musical and psychoanalytic themes, aural definition of characters, emotional power, and compositional brilliance.

I emphasize once again that one does not need formal training in music in order to affectively experience Bernstein's creative use of the formal language of music. In "The Tonight Ensemble," we *hear* musical polyphony through harmonic dissonances, clashing tonalities, and multiple rhythms; these elements provide an aural analogue for the characters' verbal expressions of latent and manifest motivations, drives and defenses. Preoedipal and oedipal themes and complex relationships are brought to the fore with full intensity. Together the varied musical elements aurally portray affects of love, hate, prejudice, jealousy, and revenge – the same affects experienced by Mr. B in the clinical illustration with which I began this case-ette.

Polyphonically, the music that introduces the ensemble – before even one word is sung – is in two keys, C major and E major, which clash with each other, analogous to the conflict of emotions experienced by the sparring gangs on stage. These contrasting tonal relationships convey harmonic dissonance, which are affectively experienced by the listener as psychic tension. Although the opening key signature is that of C major, the bass line includes G sharp and F sharp – notes found in E major, among other keys, but not in C major. This clashes with the simultaneous G natural played by other instruments. Further, two time signatures (governing the number of beats per measure) are indicated, with four beats per measure alternating with two beats per measure, drawing attention to the composer's use of rhythmic multi-dimensionality (p. 115, vocal score, Boosey and Hawkes).

The music itself, i.e., the sonic "data," creates an edgy atmosphere before Riff begins to sing the words, "The Jets are gon-na have their day … to-night," and Bernardo adds, "The Sharks are gon-na have their way … tonight" (p. 115). As the ensemble progresses, "wrong"-sounding notes are injected into the melody (i.e., notes in different, or poly-, tonalities).

Anita enters with "An-i-ta's gon-na get her kicks … tonight" (pp. 119–20), sung in triplet rhythm rather than in the eighth- and sixteenth-note meter assigned to the other Sharks. The alteration in her rhythm but not in her polytonality (which is in both C and E major) sets off her sultry, sexy agenda. Her motivation appears to be erotic, but her refrain is composed in the same two tonalities used by the male gang members, who threaten to "cut [each other] down to size" (p. 117).

Tony joins in subsequently in the key of A major, reprising his wistful and loving "Tonight" melody, which modulates to C major (the key center of both the Sharks and the Jets), and then back to A major – but with incidental F naturals in the bass. These F naturals could be interpreted to connote latent tension in Tony's refrain because they are not part of his key of A major (p. 121).

The ensemble concludes on a C major chord, but this is preceded by several measures of an unusual harmonic pattern: a series of C major, D major, and E flat major chords heard over an *ostinato* (repeated note pattern) of A flats and E flats in the bass line. This is definitely not traditional in classical music's canon of key relationships. Consequently, as we listen, our ears and psyches become attuned to the unsettling notion that "something's coming" later in the show (p. 130).

Figure 7.1 Polytonal and polyrhythmic opening of the Tonight Ensemble in *West Side Story* by Leonard Bernstein

Consider the idea that the longings, hopes, tensions, and ambiguities conveyed in this music are alive not only *within each character on stage,* but also, by extension, *within each listener in the audience* – reflecting our own polyphonic mental processes and dynamically fluctuating affects. Consider that all the Sharks and Jets – and we as listeners – viscerally experience Bernstein's aural conveyance of musical and mental complexities. The *formal balance* of the *musical* elements in "The Tonight Ensemble" resonates with our own mental counterpoint. Bernstein's compositional creativity, expressed within the formal properties of music, provides the listener with the means to cope with psychic complexities and ambiguities.

Intrapsychic, interpersonal, and social forces are all part of the psychic and sonic polyphony in *West Side Story.* The manifest and latent messages conveyed through Bernstein's use of a musical vocabulary can be conceptualized as aural analogues of psychoanalytic perspectives. *West Side Story* bridges music and mind, stage and couch.

Music's nonverbal language compels us to struggle with the elevating and disquieting dynamics that all of us share and provides us with the opportunity to do some intrapsychic work in sorting them out. Listeners in the theater and concert hall, not unlike patients in our consulting rooms, are "challenged to take part in the very process of 'working through' the artistic message" (Noy, 2009, p. 4). The music speaks for itself and for each of us.

PART III

The aural/oral road less traveled

Chapter 8

Beyond the concert hall and consulting room

As I begin this final chapter, I am reminded of a question posed to me many years ago in an oral examination for my doctorate. I was enthusiastically expounding upon the relationship between personality, social factors, and career choice in music. I recall my surprise, shock, and confusion when my advisor, Jesse Gordon, interrupted and asked, "Why would anyone be interested in this information?" I had assumed the answer to that was obvious! After regaining my composure, however, I realized that my advisor was asking me to think about *why* my dissertation topic was important to anyone else but me, and how one could *make use of* the theoretical ideas I was extolling.

That scene and my feelings at the time have remained intact in my memory, and they return to my mind now. Why should anyone be interested or care if music and psychoanalytic concepts inform each other? How is this information useful?

An intersection

Composers and performers have historically and currently set precedents in extending their formal work beyond the perimeters of the concert hall. In doing so, they have evoked affects, influenced cultural trends, effected educational reform, changed social policy, and, perhaps unknowingly, illustrated psychoanalytic principles. A few examples of interdisciplinary overlappings that pertain to the music cited in the case-ettes will be highlighted here. Clearly, other composers and musical styles have contributed to social, cultural, educational, psychological, and political discourse as well.

Mozart held membership in the Illuminati branch of the Freemasons, who promoted the ideals of enlightenment and humanism – themes that appear as sonic motives in some of his music. The Freemasons maintained that certain musical expressions represented specific Masonic signs and meanings. For example, their initiation ceremony began with the candidate knocking three times at the door to seek entry. Musically, this is expressed in three repeated chords in the overture in Mozart's opera *The Magic Flute.* And according to Thomson (1977), there are many other examples of specific musical symbols taken from the Masonic rites that appear throughout Mozart's compositions. These include the use of musical suspensions to indicate friendship and brotherhood, and of three-part harmony to metaphorically emphasize the importance of the number three in Freemasonry. Other notational devices signify the Masonic ideals of courage and resilience.

As budget cuts challenge the scope of the arts in the United States today, it is interesting to revisit another time and place when political policies similarly threatened the performing arts. In Italy during Giuseppe Verdi's lifetime (1813–1901), Italian opera in particular was under fire. By the late 1860s, the Italian government had eliminated funding for orchestras and theaters, yet insisted on taxing box office receipts. Verdi advocated for the repeal of the government box office tax and for subsidy of opera in Milan, Rome, and Naples. He lobbied for the government to pay a salary to members of orchestras and choruses.

In 1874, in a newly united Italy, Verdi was made a senator for life. In this capacity, he spoke out in favor of financing the arts and opera companies and of providing education in music for a broader range of students, including girls. One of his final projects was the construction of a rest home for musicians in Milan, where he himself was buried in 1901 at age eighty-seven. At the composer's funeral, in front of a large gathering, the thirty-four-year-old Arturo Toscanini conducted a choir of nine hundred singers in *"Va, pensiero"* from Verdi's opera *Nabucco*. It was *Nabucco,* with its famous chorus of Hebrew slaves, that approximately sixty years earlier had established Verdi as a major composer. Equally poignant, this opera cemented Verdi's reputation as a beloved champion of Italian patriots seeking unity and freedom from foreign control.

Sergei Prokofiev and his contemporary Russian composer colleagues could not avoid being affected by politics. Following the Bolshevik Revolution in October 1917, the Communist state controlled the arts, and initially they flourished. By the end of the 1920s, however, Stalin's regime had begun to insist that the arts promote particular ideologies. In 1918, Prokofiev left Russia to establish a career in the United States and Western Europe. He returned to his homeland in 1936, the year he wrote *Peter and the Wolf* with its possible autobiographical content and its political/psychological, multiply determined latent undertones about capturing a wolf. (The wolf could be understood as a metaphor for a Communist leader, for the composer's impulses and defenses, and/or for a young boy coming of age, depending on one's point of view.)

Peter and the Wolf was considered a tuneful work for the masses and was endorsed by the controlling party. However, by 1948, Prokofiev, along with Dmitri Shostakovich and Aram Khachaturian, had come under criticism from the government. Prokofiev wrote a letter to the "Assembly of Composers" apologizing for his music, claiming that he had been influenced by Western ideas and musical atonality, but it is unclear whether this "confession" was sincere. Was it merely a coincidence that, in 1948, Prokofiev's estranged Jewish wife was arrested, charged with spying, and sentenced to eight years of labor in Siberia?

It is not possible to know how the formal qualities of music provoked condemnation and/or led to approval of these composers by the state, but it is clear that the Soviet leaders were affected by music and its emotional power, and thus attempted to dictate music's impact on political and social doctrine. Through music's nonverbal language, composers could and did acquiesce to or defy dictators who applied their own unique interpretations to nonverbal sounds for political purposes. The melodies in the minds of many Soviet composers during this dark era were sometimes believed to convey manifest loyalty, but they also served as personal creative outlets for the expression of latent commentary and beliefs involving struggles for freedom. Ironically, two voices, highly influential in different ways, were silenced on March 5, 1953, when Sergei Prokofiev and Joseph Stalin died on the same day.

In 1986, Leonard Bernstein, a 1939 graduate of Harvard University, delivered a speech at his alma mater on the occasion of the University's three hundred and fiftieth anniversary. The historical moment was alive with fears of terrorism and political deception. According to historian Oja and biographer Horowitz (2008), Pan Am Flight 73 had just been hijacked and terrorist bombings had erupted in Paris. Threats had accompanied Bernstein's tour with the Israel Philharmonic when he conducted in Vienna shortly after Kurt Waldheim, a former intelligence officer for the Nazis, was elected president. But Bernstein refused to boycott the Vienna Philharmonic, preferring to seek a solution for compromise through music and his artistic ambassadorship.

On the day before Bernstein's Harvard presentation, reporter Bernard Kalb resigned from the State Department at the *New York Times* to protest its deceptive campaign against ousting Moammar Gadhafi. In the margins of his personal copy of the *New York Times* article about Kalb, Bernstein wrote in capital letters: "ENEMIES ARE OBSOLETE" (Oja and Horowitz, 2008, p. 72).

In his Harvard speech, "Truth in Time of War," several of Bernstein's comments emerge as politically passionate and psychoanalytically insightful. In speaking about the "enemy," Bernstein declares:

> I had never before been so aware of the metaphorical being, The Enemy; but the more protection one has, the more danger is implied; the stronger the defense, the greater must be the threat. At one point I suddenly realized that this is the way the world lives, is practiced in living – existing in terms of an enemy. It's exactly the target that Jesus aimed at all his life, and Buddha too, and Freud; and Gandhi and Martin Luther King: trying to make this invisible creature unnecessary.
>
> (Oja and Horowitz, 2008, p. 75)

Bernstein's political and personal views on compromise between intractable philosophies, cultures, and internal enemies were conveyed musically in his masterpiece *West Side Story*, composed twenty-nine years before his 1986 Harvard lecture. The diabolical and ambiguous tritone and the formal musical techniques of polyphony used in *West Side Story* powerfully illustrate the dynamics and vicissitudes of numerous psychoanalytic concepts and of themes embedded in history and society, as well as in our individual psyches and our interpersonal relationships. *West Side Story*'s manifest message is bold and its latent message is timeless.

In contemplating *West Side Story* from a psycho/socio/historical framework, I associate with Freud's pessimistic and cautionary statement in *Civilization and Its Discontents* (1930):

> The element of truth … which people are so ready to disavow, is that men are not gentle creatures who want to be loved, and who at the most can defend themselves if they are attacked; they are, on the contrary, creatures among whose instinctual endowments is to be reckoned a powerful share of aggressiveness. As a result, their neighbor is for them not only a potential helper or sexual object, but also someone who tempts them to satisfy their aggressiveness on him, to exploit his capacity for work without compensation, to use him sexually without his consent, to seize his possessions, to humiliate him, to cause him pain, to torture and to kill him. Homo homini lupus. Who, in the face of all his experience of life and of history, will have the courage to dispute this assertion?
>
> (*S. E.,* vol. XXI, p. 111)

Clearly, Freud's comments express his beliefs about the world at war, but also those about warring elements within the mind, as he reflects back upon his own remarkable era. Have we gone back to the future in the tumultuous early years of the twenty-first century, as Freud's theory about repetition compulsion would suggest? Certainly, both psychoanalysts and musicians can contribute meaningfully to sociopolitical commentary, both about world events and about inner life.

As developed by Freud, psychoanalysis is a theory and a treatment of mental functioning. Initially ensconced in university medical schools in the United States, it has not been fully integrated within curricula in the humanities and liberal arts. Burgeoning contemporary fields of neuroscience, psychopharmacology, and other psychological models, particularly cognitive behavior therapy, have gradually eroded psychoanalytic endorsement and inclusion in the curricula at institutions of higher learning. How farsighted and inclusive Freud was to advocate that psychoanalytic instruction should include

> branches of knowledge which are remote from medicine, and which the doctor does not come across in his practice; the history of civilization, mythology, the psychology of religion and the science of literature. Unless he is well at home in these subjects, an analyst can make nothing of a large amount of his material. By way of compensation, the great mass of what is taught in medical schools is of no use to him for his purposes.
>
> (1926, p. 246, cited in Wallerstein, 2011, pp. 629–30)

Yet didn't Freud overlook a broader scope of psychoanalytic application and interdisciplinary collaboration when, for whatever reasons, he discounted music? Both psychoanalytic and musical perspectives have much to offer beyond theoretical and formal applications in addressing contemporary complexities.

In the young decades of the twenty-first century, we have seen a loss of emphasis on internal life and latent meanings in our extraordinarily tumultuous social, political, artistic, and economic milieu. Highly charged, anti-collaborative political climates shaping health care reform; medical insurance companies' denials and limits of mental health claims; social, economic, and political unrest; and global terrorism continue to take their toll. In addition, graying concert goers, diminished overall attendance at classical arts events, restrictive health insurance policies, illusions of medication magic, and demands for quick fixes for longstanding emotional and social problems have had far-reaching effects on American society and around the globe.

In mental health care, clinical specialties have congregated in their respective corners of cognitive behavioral theory and its derivatives, psychodynamic theory and its derivatives, pharmacology, and neuroscience. Many, if not most, American university psychology and psychiatry departments have jettisoned and/or minimized emphasis on psychodynamic theories in favor of biopsychological, psychiatric, and cognitive approaches (see Kernberg, 2011; Sonnenberg, 2011; Wallerstein, 2011). Popular trends in media reporting, celebrity worship, and instant access to Internet wisdom accentuate simplicity, quick answers, and sound bites. Prudence Gourguechon (2011) calls this a "public health crisis ... a national emergency of superficiality, of simplification of cause and effect, and of ignoring or trivializing the inner life" (p. 448). I concur and call the "trivializing of inner life" a crisis in creative and critical thinking.

Classical music, like psychoanalysis, faces challenges. For the classical performing musician, the job market in the United States is more problematic than for many other highly skilled and well-educated professionals. Unemployment in the arts has typically been high, the pay often inadequate, and many musicians work at jobs considerably below the level of their accomplishments. The January 2010 National Endowment for the Arts research report on artist unemployment rates for 2008 and 2009 – which included all artists, but specifically musicians – showed sustained, high levels of unemployment. In fact, unemployment rose faster during this period for the artist population than for the civilian workforce. And in 2008 and 2009, artists of all types left the workforce altogether in greater numbers than did others in the general population.

These data contribute to a significant factor in the 2008 economic recession in the United States and its aftershock, the international stock market rollercoaster. Individuals pursuing careers in the arts – who have typically undergone specialized, intense, and highly skilled training in early childhood to achieve professional status in adulthood – have been profoundly affected both emotionally and financially. Psychoanalysts, who have undertaken lengthy, intense training and post-professional degrees, have been no less immune to the far-reaching ravaging and negative effects of the economic downturn.

While it is not my intention here to explore contemporary crises in mental health, society, economics, politics, arts, and education, my thoughts about music and psychoanalysis are influenced by my surroundings, my background, and my interests. My doctoral advisor's question about the usefulness of theoretical constructs remains as relevant today as does the query of my music theory teacher at Juilliard – who, after I had formally analyzed in meticulous detail the ambiguous opening chord of *Tristan and Isolde,* asked me, "But how does it *sound?*" As a psychoanalyst, I add: "And what does it *mean?*"

A *New York Times* front page article about Freud's death on September 26, 1939, acknowledged that "his ideas … already permeate our culture and language." Fast-forwarding seventy-two years, Kernberg (2011) recently reiterated that sentiment, and added a proviso: "Psychoanalysis has been accepted as a major contribution to the culture of the twentieth century, but its future role as a science and a profession is uncertain and being challenged" (p. 609).

In concluding this chapter and this book, I pay homage to the wisdom and curiosity of my doctoral advisor and my Juilliard teacher about why psychoanalytic and musical concepts are so important, and also how they may be useful in nontraditional settings. In doing so, I emphasize the significance of mental life both *inside* and *outside* the consulting room and the concert hall. Here at a twenty-first-century crossroad, there is now a window of opportunity for the development of interdisciplinary intersections on both aural and oral roads.

In this climate, the vestiges of deeply held convictions and controversies that compartmentalize clinical psychoanalytic practice and classical music concertizing as the gold standard in their respective disciplines can finally be put to rest. Psychoanalytic and musical knowledge can contribute in many areas that impact human motivation, critical thinking, and our quality of life, while probing beneath external events and simplistic solutions to thorny psychological questions. Responsible and informed musical and psychoanalytic ambassadors, through writing, speaking, performing, and teaching can educate and advocate in a variety of arenas. Such ambassadors can provide in-depth perspectives about the human condition, about powerful affects and unconscious motivations, and can share multiply determined views on complex topics such as gender, poverty, war, racism, oppression, immigration, and child and adult development. Love, hate, anger, envy, grief, and other intense affects that fuel anxiety and depression, when unattended, can ferment and be acted upon unproductively and sometimes dangerously. Both musical and psychoanalytic knowledge can help us deal with this challenge in ourselves and with others.

The manifest and latent lessons and affects illustrated in musical and psychoanalytic perspectives in *Peter and the Wolf, Otello, Lucia di Lammermoor,* Mozart's A Minor Piano Sonata, K. 310, and *West Side Story* speak to a broad, creative application of music and psychoanalytic theory and practice. For example, in designing educational programs for teachers, parents, caregivers, policymakers, and students, why not use *Peter and the Wolf* to illustrate nuanced concepts about child development? Why not mine *West Side Story* to creatively convey the tragedy of soul murder (see Shengold, 1989) and the displacement of self-hate involved in bullying, as well as to show how underlying rage and alienation can explode into violent actions? Programs that draw upon the music and the background of Mozart's Piano Sonata in A Minor, K. 310, can be developed to help individuals and communities cope with grief and loss – applicable to so many people in today's post-9/11 society who have lost loved ones, jobs, and homes.

We know that natural disasters such as the 2011 Japanese earthquake and tsunami, and Hurricanes Katrina and Irene in the United States, leave massive individual and societal devastation in their wake. To help us cope with these natural disasters and the intrapsychic and interpersonal tragedies they cause, we can turn to an appreciation of the portrayal of ambiguity, jealousy, heartbreak, and psychic breakdown in *Otello,* and of the psychic forces that can overwhelm the ego's ability to cope in *Lucia di Lammermoor.* Further, these two powerful works, as well as *West Side Story,* speak to the oppression brought about by ruthlessness, by dysfunctional families, and, by extension, to power and political stalemates in our own country and abroad. The ongoing crises of oppression in the Middle East and elsewhere, and the present political/ economic gridlock in the United States, are but further examples of situations in which people can lose hope and then resort to unproductive and/or destructive actions – themes that are again pertinent to the messages of *Lucia di Lammermoor, Otello,* and *West Side Story*.

An example comes to mind of a collaborative undertaking in which music and psychology have been successfully and creatively blended, as recommended here: El Sistema USA and its Abreu Fellows. Now established worldwide in education and in social service agencies, this program began with only eleven music students and grew into an energetic system of teaching music to three hundred thousand of Venezuela's poorest children, to enhance self-esteem.

It has been demonstrated that musical study and performance can transform individuals and their communities by increasing self-knowledge and self-esteem, a core goal of psychoanalysis. Why not include topics that encourage insights into music in psychoanalytic training and educational programs, as well as develop courses about the psychology of performance and outreach in musical curricula, particularly at the university level? Such collaborations between musicians and psychoanalysts provide unique opportunities for deepening sensitivities, increasing interdisciplinary interactions, and benefiting both individuals and communities. The ways to creatively draw upon music and psychoanalytic concepts are limited only by one's imagination.

While I have illustrated specific music and psychoanalytic concepts in my case-ettes, what I emphasize here are not specific compositions or psychoanalytic theories, but the importance of finding creative ways to engage in public dialogue and education on all levels through a collaborative lens of psychoanalytic and musical frameworks. This approach does not lessen the importance of clinical practice or musical performance venues, of course, since these can also play a role in loosening the stalemates that all too often impede personal, social, political, and cultural discourse and emotional growth. That music and psychoanalytic ideas, singly or in convergence, can be useful outside the consulting room and the concert hall does not require an apology to the classical canon of either discipline.

At a crossroad

Economic, cultural, educational, and social conundrums present challenges intermingled with opportunities in our time as well as in the eras of our psychoanalytic and music ancestors. Attention to multifaceted dynamics that broaden and deepen the understanding of complex issues is compatible with critical thinking and with reflection about the counterpoint beneath mental melodies. Music and psychoanalytic concepts have held their value over time; they beg for innovative application both within and outside their formal edifices, offices, and universities, thereby transcending theoretical constructs and clinical applications. Analysts and musicians can be proactive in playing educational roles in an era of changing perceptions and misinformed projections about both classical music and psychoanalytic ideas, so that what is valuable does not become vulnerable.

In describing a new model for education, Steven Levy emphasizes that psychoanalytic knowledge has

> crucial relevance in myriad settings ... Only one is the world of therapeutics .... By psychoanalytic knowledge, I refer broadly to our knowledge about human behavior viewed from the perspectives of rationality and irrationality, conscious and unconscious mental determinants, conflict and compromise, and lifelong developmental adaptation.
>
> (2009, p. 1302)

Regarding music settings, Alex Ross (2010) suggests a strategy of performing classical concerts in nontraditional venues such as nightclubs, where musicians also talk informally with audiences. Demographic data from the National Endowment for the Arts (2010) show that both urban and rural populations "share an appetite for ... cultural expression" (p. 11), which has led to the scheduling of appealing programs for varied populations in unusual but accessible locations. These settings include shopping malls, coffee shops, places of worship, and schools.

It was Ernst Ticho's (1973) vision to extend "what psychoanalysts have learned from individuals to groups and communities" (p. 1). I concur with

Ticho, as well as with Stuart Twemlow (2009), who sees a "major potential leadership role for psychoanalysts in the solution of community and social problems" (p. 93). Political involvement provides another forum in which psychoanalysts and musicians can collaborate. A recent example occurred in Rome, Italy, during the observance of the one hundred and fiftieth anniversary of Italy's unification (Ross, 2011).

Similar to what has happened in the United States, where budgetary cuts to the arts threaten our cultural heritage, the Italian government has recently slashed its budget for the arts. How moving that Verdi's chorus "Va, pensiero" from *Nabucco*, which became the patriots' rallying cry for a united Italy in Verdi's time is relevant once more in Italy as the survival of the arts is threatened once again in the very birthplace of opera. How poignant that the nationalist slogan *"Viva Vittorio Emanuele, Re d'Italia"* (Long live Victor Emmanuel, King of Italy) was hidden from the Austrian enemy by its acronym *"Viva VERDI,"* which also acknowledged the beloved composer Giuseppe Verdi. How powerful that when the chorus sang "Va, pensiero" at the Rome Opera in the summer of 2011, someone yelled, "Viva l'Italia," leading conductor Riccardo Muti to address the audience, repeat the beloved chorus, and invite them to join in (Ross, 2011).

Despite having previously stated, "You can't eat culture," shortly after this event, Italy's finance minister adjusted the earlier budgetary cuts to the arts, and the prime minister, amidst public displays of disapproval, attended a performance of *Nabucco*. It is interesting that this shift in policy occurred in the wake of a convergence of music and deep nationalism, fueled by affective reminiscence and resonance to the music and meaning of "Va, pensiero." The profound longing for connection to one's motherland, one's home, and one's roots, which expresses deeply psychoanalytic themes, was evoked musically. Music itself, musical advocacy, and its latent, unspoken, but heard and deeply felt psychoanalytic implications resulted in a political action that affected Italians and effected public policy.

I applaud Isaac Tylim (2009), who advocates for the development of a psychoanalytic attitude toward cultural institutions. Tylim maintains that:

> At the turn of the twenty-first century, the need for psychoanalytic contribution to the global community has ceased to be considered a violation of analytic neutrality, and applied psychoanalysis is in the process of losing its status as step-child of our discipline .... September 11 brought the psychoanalyst's couch onto the streets, the piers, and the shelter.
>
> (2009, p. 95)

Here Tylim is describing the adoption of a psychoanalytic perspective toward intolerance, problem solving, negotiating, and compromise regarding international affairs in institutions such as the United Nations. Programs based on a psychoanalytic understanding of prejudice and aggression, for example, if implemented at the UN and elsewhere, may result in new "enlightened partnerships" (2009, p. 97).

The gun lobbyists' argument that "guns don't kill people, people kill people" can be heard as a warning of the need to address underlying interpersonal and intrapsychic issues that beset persons who resort to violent action, using weapons to express disillusionment, rejection, desperation, and rage; we hear this musically in such works as *Lucia di Lammermoor, Otello,* and *West Side Story,* as has been noted. After the 1998 killing of two security guards at the Capitol in Washington, DC, I suggested that we need "better *mental detection,* instead of erecting more *metal detectors* in federal buildings," in attempts to avert violence, and to identify and treat emotional problems (Nagel, 1998b). Sadly, as this book is in its final stage of edits, once more we are coping with lingering questions and psychic pain in the aftermath of the brutal, senseless killing of innocent people in a movie theater in Aurora, Colorado. It is time to reconceptualize the clichéd phrase *outreach* as literally *reaching out* and *going out* into the community, beyond our comfort zones and our psychoanalytic and musical choirs, and beyond our offices, our institutes, and our concert halls, to collaborate with others formally, informally, and meaningfully.

A convergence

The royal road to the unconscious has converged – rather than diverged – at an *aural* and *oral* intersection that links music and psychoanalysis. On this road, there is a junction between the psychoanalytic couch and the concert stage – within the larger community of ideas. I do not think it is too far a leap to suggest that the music conceptualized as quasi-psychoanalytic data in my case-ettes, as well as many other compositions not mentioned, transcends the proscenium of the stage, the concert hall, and the orchestra pit.

Similarly, theory (theories) that informs (inform) psychotherapy in the privacy of the consulting room has (have) broader application beyond the proverbial couch. The intersection of music (and all the arts) with psychoanalysis can be enhanced by the development of imaginative interdisciplinary programs. Such programs can embrace educators, musicians, community organizers, social service workers, social media, police departments, government officials, economists, journalists, health care providers, and many others.

To quote and elaborate the remarks of Joseph Polisi, president of the Juilliard School:

> Artists [*and analysts*] of the twenty-first century, especially in America, must re-dedicate themselves to a broader professional agenda that reaches beyond what has been expected of them in an earlier time …. These artists [*and analysts*] must be not only communicative through their art, but also be knowledgeable about the intricacies of our society – politically, economically, socially – so that they can effectively work toward showing

the power of the arts [*and of psychoanalytic ideas*] to a nation and its people who are often uninformed … and view these activities with suspicion, occasional disdain, and frequently as being irrelevant.

(2005, p. 11, italics added by JJN to include analysts and psychoanalytic ideas)

Music is an essential instrument in my psychoanalytic repertoire. I believe that music successfully "illuminates elements of the underlying structures of the mind" (Feder, 1993b, p. 4). Returning to the genius of Leonard Bernstein, I suggest that his conscious and unconscious sensitivity to musical, intrapsychic, interpersonal, and social complexities in *West Side Story* can be conceptualized as an intersection of musical theory and theories of mind. This holds implications for clinical practice, and can transport psychoanalytic concepts multi-directionally between the analytic couch, the Broadway stage, the concert hall, and the community. The connections between musical and psychoanalytic concepts provide an elegant schema for thinking about the counterpoint of an individual's inner world as that world interacts with social "reality."

While caution is advised against oversimplifying any implication that intellectual understanding leads to insight, and warnings are issued about reckless interpretation using music as a symbolic function of the mind, I emphasize that responses to artistic creations can have a mutative impact on the understanding of self and other. When using a poem illustratively as a form of interpretation and "therapy," Schafer (1992) suggests that the "reader becomes a co-author of the text" (just as he has argued), and "the analyst may be considered a co-author of the analysand's text …. It can be argued that the poem changes with the reader …. It is no longer the same poem" (p. 184). I maintain that this occurs with music, in various ways, for the listener as well as for the performer and the composer. That music and psychoanalysis contribute powerfully to thinking, feeling, understanding, and the creation of meaning is a lasting legacy for both disciplines. In that regard, music and psychoanalysis remain perpetually relevant and resilient in our psychic and musical repertoires. Both disciplines, now more than ever, rely on our ingenuity, boldness, and resourcefulness to promote their enduring and endearing values.

Bibliography

Abraham, K. (1914). The Ear and Auditory Passage as Erotogenic Zones, in *Selected Papers on Psychoanalysis* (1942). London: Hogarth, pp. 244–7.

Abrams, D. M. (1993). Freud and Max Graf: On the Psychoanalysis of Music, in S. Feder, R. L. Karmel, and G. H. Pollock (eds), *Psychoanalytic Explorations in Music* (Second Edition). Madison, CT: International Universities Press, pp. 279–307.

Adorno, T. (1952). *In Search of Wagner* (trans. R. Livingstone). UK: Thetford Press Ltd.

Anderson, E. (1938). *The Letters of Mozart and His Family* (First Edition; in three volumes). London: Macmillan.

Anderson, E. (1966) *The Letters of Mozart and His Family* (Second Edition; in two volumes), (completed by A. Hyatt King and Monica Carolan). London, Melbourne, Toronto: Macmillan and New York: St Martin's Press.

Anderson, E. (1938). *The Letters of Mozart and His Family* (Second Edition), (two vols), completed by A. Hyatt King and Monica Carolan. London: Macmillan.

Anzieu, D. (1975). *Freud's Self-analysis* (trans. P. Graham). Madison, CT: International Universities Press, 1986.

Anzieu, D. (1976). L'enveloppe Sonore du Sio, *Nouv. Rev. Psychanal.*, 13: 161–77. (The Sound Image of the Self, *International Review of Psychoanalysis*, 6: 23–6.)

Ashbrook, W. (1982). *Donizetti and His Operas*. Cambridge: Cambridge University Press.

Barale, F. (1997). Figure dell'anima. Appunti Su Arte, Psicopatolgia, Pscicoanalisi (Figures of the Soul. Notes on Art, Psychotherapy, and Psychoanalysis), in *Figure dell'anima. Arte Irregolare in Europa*. Milan: Mazzotta, pp. 26–34.

Barale, F. and Minazzi, V. (2008). Off the Beaten Track: Freud, Sound and Music. Statement of a Problem and Some Historico-critical Notes, *International Journal of Psychoanalysis,* 89 (5), October: 937–57.

Bardas, W. (1919). Zur Problematik der Music, *Imago*, 5: 364–71.

Baudry, F. (1984). An Essay on Method in Applied Psychoanalysis, *Psychoanalytic Quarterly*, 53: 551–81.

Beattie, H. J. (2005). *Revenge: Panel Report*, Winter Meeting, APsaA, New York, January 24, 2004, *Journal of the American Psychoanalytic Association*, 53 (2): 513–34.

Bernays, A. F. (1940). My Brother, Sigmund Freud, in H. M. Ruitenbeck (ed.), *Freud As We Knew Him*. Detroit: Wayne State University Press, pp. 140–7.

Bernstein, L., Sondheim, S., Laurents, A., and Robbins, J. (1957, 1958, 2000) *West Side Story* (vocal score). Milwaukee, WI: Leonard Bernstein Music Publishing Company LLC, Boosey & Hawkes, Hal Leonard Corporation, ISBN 0-634-04678-0.

Bernstein, L., Sondheim, S., Laurents, A., and Robbins, J. (1994). *West Side Story* (engraved orchestral score). The Amberson Group, Inc., Boosey & Hawkes, Inc. (estate of Leonard Bernstein). New York and London.

Bettelheim, B. (1989). *The Uses of Enchantment: The Meaning and Importance of Fairy Tales*. New York: Vintage Books.

Botstein, L. (1999). Schoenberg and the Audience: Modernism, Music and Politics in the Twentieth Century, in W. Frisch (ed.), *Schoenberg and His World*. Princeton, NJ: Princeton University Press, pp. 19–54.

Brakel, L.A.W. (2002). Phantasy and Wish: A Proper Function Account of a-Rational Primary Process Mediated Mentation, *Australasian Journal of Philosophy*, 80 (1): 1–16.

— — (2003). Unusual Human Experiences: Kant, Freud and an Associationist Law, *Theoria et Historia Scientiarum*, VII (2): 109–16.

——(2004). The Psychoanalytic Assumption of the Primary Process: Extra-psychoanalytic Evidence and Findings, *Journal of the American Psychoanalytic Association*, 52 (1): 131–61.

— — (2007). Music and Primary Process: Proposal for a Preliminary Experiment, *American Imago* (The Aural Road Edition), 64 (1): 37–57.

Brenner, C. (2006). *Psychoanalysis or Mind and Meaning*. New York: The Psychoanalytic Quarterly, Inc.

Burton, H. (1994). *Leonard Bernstein*. New York, NY: Doubleday.

Cattell, R. B. and Anderson, J. C. (1954). Musical Preferences and Personality Diagnosis: A Factorization of One Hundred and Twenty Themes, *Journal of Social Psychology*, 39: 3–24.

Cheshire, N. M. (1996). The Empire of the Ear: Freud's Problem with Music, *International Journal of Psycho-Analysis*, 77: 1127–68.

Chijs, van der, A. (1923). An Attempt to Apply Objective Psychoanalysis to Musical Composition (abstract), *International Journal of Psychoanalysis*, 4: 379–80.

Chijs, van der, A. (1926). Uber as Unisono in er Komposition, *Imago,* 12: 23–31.

Cooper, A. M. (2005). *The Quiet Revolution in American Psychoanalysis*. Rome and New York: Brunner-Routledge.

Copland, A. (1957). *What to Listen for in Music*. New York: McGraw Hill Book Company.

Diaz de Chumaceiro, C. L. (1993). Richard Wagner's Life and Music: What Freud Knew, in S. Feder, R. L. Karmel, and G. H. Pollock (eds), *Psychoanalytic Explorations in Music* (Second Edition). Madison, CT: International Universities Press, pp. 249–78.

Donizetti, G. (1898, renewed 1926). *Lucia di Lammermoor*, Opera Score Editions. New York: G. Schirmer.

Drabkin, W. (2001). Tritone, in S. Ladie and J. Tyrrell (eds), *The New Grove Dictionary of Music and Musicians* (Second Edition). London: Macmillan, Volume 25, pp. 747–9.

Ehrenzweig, A. (1953). *The Psychoanalysis of Artistic Vision and Hearing*. New York: George Braziller.

Ehrenzweig, A. (1975). *The Psychoanalysis of Artistic Vision and Hearing* (Third Edition). London: Shelton Press.

Einstein, A. (1945). *Mozart: His Character and His Work* (trans. Arthur Mendel and Nathan Broder). New York: Oxford University Press.

Epstein, D. (1993). On Affect and Musical Motion, in S. Feder, R. Karmel, and G. Pollock (eds), *Psychoanalytic Explorations of Music*. Madison, CT: International Universities Press, pp. 91–123.

Feder, S. (1983). *The Enduring Father: Psychoanalysis in Ives Studies*. Presentation to the American Musicological Society, Louisville, KY.

— — (1990a). George and Charles Ives: the Veneration of Boyhood, in S. Feder, R. L. Karmel, and G. H. Pollock (eds), (1990). *Psychoanalytic Explorations in Music*. Madison, CT: International Universities Press, pp. 115–76.

— — (1990b). The Nostalgia of Charles Ives: An Essay in Affects and Music, in S. Feder, R. L. Karmel, and G. H. Pollock (eds), (1990). *Psychoanalytic Explorations in Music*. Madison, CT: International Universities Press, pp. 233–66.

— — (1992). *Charles Ives "My Father's Song" (A Psychoanalytic Biography)*. New Haven and London: Yale University Press.

— — (1993a). Mozart in D minor – or, The Father's Blessing; The Father's Curse, in P. Ostwald and L. S. Zegans (eds), *The Pleasure and Perils of Genius: Mostly Mozart*. Madison, CT: International Universities Press, pp. 117–31.

— — (1993b). "Promissory Notes": Method in Music and Applied Psychoanalysis, in S. Feder, R. L. Karmel, and G. H. Pollock (eds), *Psychoanalytic Explorations in Music*. Madison, CT: International Universities Press, pp. 3–19.

— — (1997). *Autobiography in Music: Music as Autobiography: An Inquiry in Method and Meaning*. Unpublished, Harvard University Colloquium, December 8, 1997.

— — (2004). *Music as Simulacrum of Mental Life*. Pre-circulated paper, winter 2004 meetings of American Psychoanalytic Association, unpublished, available at internationalpsychoanlaysis.net

Feder, S., Karmel, R. L., and Pollock, G. H. (eds) (1990). *Psychoanalytic Explorations in Music*. Madison, CT: International Universities Press.

Feder, S., Karmel, R. L., and Pollock, G. H. (eds) (1993). *Psychoanalytic Explorations in Music (Second Series)*. Madison, CT: International Universities Press.

Fisher, B. D. (2003). *Donizetti's Lucia di Lammermoor: Opera Classics Library*. Coral Gables, Florida: Opera Journeys Publishing.

Freud, S. (1900). *The Interpretation of Dreams*, S.E. IV/V (The Standard Edition of the Complete Psychological Works (SE); trans. from the German under the General Editorship of James Strachey, in collaboration with Anna Freud, assisted by Alix Strachey and Alan Tyson). London: The Hogarth Press.

— — (1905) Three Essays on Sexuality. S.E. VII: 125–245.

— — (1909a) Analysis of a Phobia in a Five-year-old Boy. S.E. X: 1–149.

— — (1909b) Addendum: Original Record of the Case (of Obsessional Neurosis). S.E. X: 253–318.

— — (1910). Leonardo Da Vinci and a Memory of his Childhood. S.E. IX: 59–137.

— — (1914a). The Moses of Michelangelo. S.E. XIII: 211–36.

— — (1914b). On Narcissism. S.E. XIV: 67–102.

— — (1915–16). Introductory Lectures on Psycho-analysis (Parts I and II). S.E. XV.

—— (1916–17). Introductory Lectures on Psycho-analysis (Part III). S.E. XVI.

—— (1917–19). An Infantile Neurosis and Other Works. S.E. XVI.

—— (1923). The Ego and the Id. S.E. XIX: 12–66.

—— (1925–26). An Autobiographical Study, Inhibitions, Symptoms and Anxiety, Lay Analysis and Other Works. S.E. XX.

—— (1927–31). Dostoevsky and Parricide (1928 [1927]). S.E. XXI: 175–96.

—— (1930). *Civilization and Its Discontents*. S.E. XXI: 64–145.

Freundlich, D. (1968). Narcissism and Exhibitionism in the Performance of Classical Music, *Psychiatric Quarterly Supplement*, 42 (1B): 1–13.

Friedman, S. M. (1960). One Aspect of the Structure of Music, *Journal of the American Psychoanalytic Association*, 8: 427–49.

Frisch, W. (1999). *Schoenberg and his World*. Princeton, NJ: Princeton University Press.

Gabbard, G. (1997). The Psychoanalyst at the Movies, *International Journal of Psychoanalysis*, 78: 429–34.

Gartenberg, E. (1978). *Mahler*. New York: Schirmer Books.

Gay, P. (1988). *Freud: A Life For Our Time*. New York: W. W. Norton and Co.

Gourguechon, P. S. (2011). The Citizen Psychoanalyst: Psychoanalysis, Social Commentary, and Social Advocacy, *Journal of the American Psychoanalytic Association*, 59 (3): 445–70.

Graf, M. (1911). Richard Wagner im Fliegenden Hollander: A Contribution to the Psychology of Artistic Creation, *Schrifen zur Angewandten Seelenkunde*, Vol. 9, 1970. Nandeln, Liechtenstein: Kraus.

—— (1942). Reminiscences of Professor Sigmund Freud, *Psychoanalytic Quarterly*, 11: 465–76.

—— (1945). *Legend of a Musical City*. New York: Philosophical Library.

—— (1957). *Every Hour Was Fulfilled: A Half-Century of Life in Music and the Theater*. Wien-Frankfurt: Forum-Verlag.

Greenacre, P. (1957). The Childhood of the Artist, *Psychoanalytic Study of the Child*, 12: 47–72.

Grinstein, A. (1992). *Conrad Ferdinand Meyer and Freud: The Beginnings of Applied Psychoanalysis*. Madison, CT: International Universities Press.

Grout, D. J. and Palisca, C. V. (1996). *A History of Western Music*. New York and London: W. W. Norton and Co.

Imberty, M. (2002) La Musica e il Bambino (Music and the Child), in J. J. Nattiez (ed.) *Encyclopaedia della Music II: Il Sapere Musicale* (Encyclopedia of Music II: Musical Knowledge). Turin: Einaudi.

Isakower, O. (1939). On the Exceptional Position of the Auditory Sphere, *International Journal of Psychoanalysis*, 20: 340–8.

Kantrowitz, Judy Leopold (2006). *Writing about Patients: Responsibilities, Risks, and Ramifications*. New York: Other Press.

Kerman, J. (1968). Verdi's Use of Recurring Themes, in H. Powers (ed.), *Studies in Music History: Essays for Oliver Strunk*. Princeton, NJ: Princeton University Press, pp. 495–509.

Kernberg, O. F. (2011). Psychoanalysis and the University: A Difficult Relationship, *International Journal of Psychoanalysis*, 92 (3): 609–22.

Klein, M. (1929). Infantile Anxiety – Situations Reflected in a Work of Art and in the Creative Impulse, *International Journal of Psychoanalysis*, 10: 436–44.

Kohut, H. (1957). Observations on the Psychological Functions of Music, *Journal of the American Psychoanalytic Association*, 5 (3): 398–407.

Kohut, H. and Levarie, S. (1950). On the Enjoyment of Listening to Music, *Psychoanalytic Quarterly*, 19: 64–87.

Kris, E. (1952). *Psychoanalytic Explorations in Art*. New York: International Universities Press.

Langer, S. K. (1942, 1957). *Philosophy in a New Key: A Study in the Symbolism of Reason, Rite, and Art*. Cambridge, MA: Harvard University Press.

— — (1953). *Feeling and Form*. New York: Charles Scribner's and Sons.

Lansky, M. R. (1992) *Fathers Who Fail: Shame and Psychopathology in the Family System*. Hillsdale, NJ: Analytic Press.

— — (2005). The Impossibility of Forgiveness: Shame Fantasies as Instigators of Vengefulness in Euripides' *Medea*, *Journal of the American Psychoanalytic Association*, 53 (2): 438–64.

— — (2007a). Discussion of Dr. Julie Nagel's paper "Psychoanalytic and Musical Perspectives on Shame in Donizetti's *Lucia di Lammermoor*". American Psychoanalytic Association 97th Annual Meeting, Denver, CO, unpublished.

— — (2007b). Jealousy and Envy in Othello: Psychoanalytic Reflections on the Rivalrous Emotions, in L. Wurmser and H. Jarass (eds), *Jealousy and Envy: New Views About Two Powerful Feelings*, Psychoanalytic Inquiry Book Series. Hillsdale, NJ: Analytic Press, pp. 25–47.

— — (2007c). Unbearable Shame, Splitting and Forgiveness in the Resolution of Vengefulness, *Journal of the American Psychoanalytic Association*, 55 (2): 571–93.

Lansky, M. R. and Morrison, A. P. (1997a). The Legacy of Freud's Writings on Shame, in M. R. Lansky and A. P. Morrison (eds), *The Widening Scope of Shame*, Hillsdale, NJ: Analytic Press, pp. 3–40.

— — (1997b). *The Widening Scope of Shame*. Hillsdale, NJ: Analytic Press.

Lawton, D. (1978). On the "Bacio" Theme in *Otello*, *19th Century Music*, 1 (3) March: 211–20.

Lee, H. B. (1947). On the Aesthetic States of the Mind, *Psychiatry*, 10 (3): 281–306.

Levy, S. (2009). Psychoanalytic Education Then and Now, *Journal of the American Psychoanalytic Association*, 57 (6) December: 1295–1309.

Lewis, H. B. (1971). *Shame and Guilt in Neurosis*. New York: International Universities Press.

Lipps, T. (1883). *Grundtatsachen des Seelenlebens*. Bonn, Germany: Cohen.

Lipson, C. (2006). The Meanings and Functions of Tunes That Come into One's Head, *Psychoanalytic Quarterly*, 75 (3): 859–78.

Lombardi, R. (2008). Time, Music, and Reverie, *Journal of the American Psychoanalytic Association*, 56 (4): 1191–1211.

— — (2009). Symmetric Frenzy and Catastrophic Change: A Consideration of Primitive Mental States in the Wake of Bion and Matte Blanco, *International Journal of Psychoanalysis*, 90 (3): 529–49.

—— (2011). The Body, Feelings, and the Unheard Music of the Senses, *Contemporary Psychoanalysis*, 47:3–24.

McDonald, M. (1970). Transitional Tunes and Musical Development, *The Psychoanalytic Study of the Child*, 25: 503–20.

Marshall, R. (1993). Bach and Mozart: Styles of Musical Genius, in S. Feder, R. L. Karmel, and G. H. Pollock (eds), *Psychoanalytic Explorations in Music (Second Series)*. Madison, CT: International Universities Press, pp. 153–69.

Martinelli, R. (2002). Affinita, ritmo, empatia. La musical nel pensiero di Th. Lip (Affinity, Rhythm, Empathy. Music in the Thought of T. Lipps), in Una "Scienza Pura della Conscienza": l'ideale della Psicologia in Theodor Lipps (A "Pure Science of Consciousness": The Idea of Psychology in Theodor Lipps), *Discipline Filosofiche*, 12: 113–32.

Masson, J. M. (ed. and trans.) (1985). *The Complete Letters of Sigmund Freud to Wilhelm Fliess* (1887–1904). Cambridge, MA: The Belknap Press/Harvard University.

Matte Blanco, I. (1981). Reflecting with Bion, in J. S. Grostein (ed.), *Do I Dare Disturb the Universe? A Memorial to Wilfred R. Bion*. Beverly Hills, CA: Caesura, pp. 489–528.

Monsonyi, D. (1935). Die Irrationalen Grundlagen der Musik, *Imago*, 21: 207–26.

Morrison, A. (1989). *Shame: The Underside of Narcissism*. Hillsdale, NJ: The Analytic Press.

Morrison, A. P. and Stolorow, R. D. (1997). Shame, Narcissism, and Intersubjectivity, in M. R. Lansky and A. P. Morrison (eds), *The Widening Scope of Shame*. Hillsdale, NJ: The Analytic Press, pp. 63–87.

Mozart, W.A., *Klaviersonaten (Band 1)* (musical score), Weiner Urtext Edition, Schott/Universal Edition (@2004), Wien, Austria.

Nagel, J. J. (1985). *The Musicians' Relationship with the Audience: Mastery or Merger*. Unpublished manuscript.

—— (1993). Stage Fright in Musicians: A Psychodynamic Perspective, *Bulletin of the Menninger Clinic*, 57 (4): 492–503.

—— (1998a). Injury and Pain in Performing Musicians: A Psychodynamic Perspective, *Bulletin of the Menninger Clinic*, 62 (1): 83–95.

—— (1998b). Power of the Mind: Taking Mental Health Seriously Would Improve Nation's Safety, *Ann Arbor News*, August 9, B7.

—— (2007). Melodies of the Mind: Mozart in 1778, *American Imago* (Aural Road Edition), 64 (1): 23–36.

—— (2008a). Psychoanalytic Perspectives on Music: An Intersection on the Oral and Aural Road, *The Psychoanalytic Quarterly*, 77 (2): 507–30.

—— (2008b). Psychoanalytic and Musical Perspectives on Shame in Donizetti's *Lucia di Lammermoor*, *Journal of the American Psychoanalytic Association*, 56 (2): 551–63.

—— (2010a). Psychoanalytic and Musical Ambiguity: The Tritone in "Gee, Officer Krupke", *Journal of the American Psychoanalytic Association*, 58 (1): 9–25.

—— (2010b). Melodies in My Mind: The Polyphony of Mental Life, *Journal of the American Psychoanalytic Association*, 58 (4) (Aug): pp. 649–62. (Gertrude and Ernst Ticho Memorial Lecture presented in Washington, D.C., June 11, 2010.)

Nagel, J. J. and Nagel, L. (2005). Animals, Music, and Psychoanalysis, in S. Akhtar and V. Volkan (eds), *Cultural Zoo: Animals in the Human Mind and its Sublimations*. Madison, CT: International Universities Press, pp. 177–206.

Nass, M. L. (1971). Some Considerations of Psychoanalytic Interpretation of Music, *Psychoanalytic Quarterly*, 40 (2): 303–16.

— — (1990). The Development of Creative Imagination in Composers, in S. Feder, R. Karmel, and G. Pollock (eds), *Psychoanalytic Explorations of Music*. Madison, CT: International Universities Press, pp. 267–83.

National Endowment for the Arts (2010). Research Note #100. March.

Noy, P. (1966). The Psychodynamics of Music, *Journal of Music Therapy*, 3 (4): 126–34.

— — (1967a). The Psychodynamics of Music, *Journal of Music Therapy*, 4 (1): 7–23.

— — (1967b). The Psychodynamics of Music, *Journal of Music Therapy*, 4 (2): 45–51.

— — (1967c). The Psychodynamics of Music, *Journal of Music Therapy*, 4 (3): 81–94.

— — (1967d). The Psychodynamics of Music, *Journal of Music Therapy*, 4 (4): 117–25.

— — (1968). The Development of Musical Ability, in S. Feder, R. Karmel and G. Pollock (eds), (1990). *Psychoanalytic Explorations of Music*. Madison, CT: International Universities Press, pp. 63–77.

— — (1993). How Music Conveys Emotion, in S. Feder, R. Karmel, and G. Pollock (eds), *Psychoanalytic Explorations of Music*. Madison, CT: International Universities Press, pp. 125–49.

— — (2009). *Art and Emotion*. Unpublished manuscript.

Oja, C. and Horowitz, M. E. (2008). Introduction: Something Called Terrorism. Speech given at Harvard University, Fall 1986, by Leonard Bernstein, *The American Scholar*: 71–79.

Ostwald, P. (1990). Johannes Brahms – Music, Loneliness, and Altruism, in S. Feder, R. Karmel, and G. Pollock (eds), *Psychoanalytic Explorations of Music*. Madison, CT: International Universities Press, pp. 291–320.

Persichetti. V. (1961). *Twentieth-century Harmony: Creative Aspects and Practice*. New York: W. W. Norton and Co.

Piers, G. and Singer, M. B. (1953). *Shame and Guilt*. New York: W. W. Norton and Co.

Polisi, J. (2005). *The Artist as Citizen*. NJ and NY: Amadeus Press.

Pratt, C. C. (1952). *Music and the Language of Emotion*. Washington, DC: US Library of Congress. (Lecture delivered under auspices of Louis Charles Elson Fund, December 21, 1950.)

Prokofieff, S. (1936, 1985). *Peter and the Wolf, Op, 67*. London: Eulenberg Ltd. Edition.

Racker, H. (1951). Contributions to Psychoanalysis of Music, *American Imago*, 8 (2): 129–63.

Reik, T. (1953). *The Haunting Melody: Psychoanalytic Experiences in Life and Music*. New York: Farrar, Straus and Young.

Rose, G. (1993). On Form and Feeling in Music, in S. Feder, R. Karmel, and G. Pollock (eds), *Psychoanalytic Explorations of Music*. Madison, CT: International Universities Press, pp. 63–81.

— — (2004). *Between Couch and Piano*. New York: Brunner-Routledge.

Rosen, C. (1996). *Arnold Schoenberg*. Chicago and London: The University of Chicago Press.

Ross, A. (2007). *The Rest is Noise*. New York: Farrar, Straus and Giroux.

— — (2010). Close Listening, *The New Yorker*, February, pp. 66–7.

— — (2011). At the Brink, *The New Yorker*, July, pp. 82–5.

Rosselli, J. (2000). *The Life of Verdi*. Cambridge: Cambridge University Press.

Sachs, H. (1945). *Freud, Master and Friend*. London: Imago Publishing.

Schafer, R. (1983). *The Analytic Attitude*. New York: Basic Books.

—— (1992). *Retelling a Life*. New York: Other Press.

—— (2003). *Insight and Interpretation*. New York: Other Press.

Schlifstein, S. I. (ed.) (1965). *Sergej Prokofjew. Dokumente, Briefe, Erinnerungen* (trans. F. Loesch). Leipzig: Deutscher Verlag fur Musik.

Schoenberg, A. (1910). "Aphorismen" in Willi Reich (ed.) (1964). *Schopferische Konfessionem*. Zurich: Peter Schifferli.

—— (1922). *Harmonielehre*, Vienna, Universal Edition (Third Edition, Vienna, Universal Edition. Originally published 1911). English translation: *Theory of Harmony* (1978) (trans. Roy E. Carter; based on the Third Edition). Berkeley and Los Angeles: University of California Press,.

Schorske, C. E. (1981). *Fin De Siecle Vienna: Politics and Culture*. New York: Vintage Books.

Scott, W. (1819). *The Bride of Lammermoor*. London: Everyman Library, 1906.

Segal, H. (1952). A Psychoanalytical Approach to Aesthetics, *International Journal of Psychoanalysis*, 33: 196–207.

Serravezza, A. (1996). *Music and Science in the Age of Positivism*. Bologna: Il Mulino.

Sharpe, E. F. (1935). Similar and Divergent Unconscious Determinants Underlying the Sublimation of Pure Art and Pure Science, *International Journal of Psychoanalysis*, 16: 186–202.

Shengold, L. (1989). *Soul Murder: The Effects of Child Abuse and Deprivation*. New Haven, CT: Yale University Press.

Slonimsky, N. (1953). *Lexicon of Musical Invective*. Seattle and London: University of Washington Press.

Smith, H. F. (2008). Leaps of Faith: Is Forgiveness a Useful Concept?, *International Journal of Psychoanalysis*, 89 (5): 919–36.

Solomon, M. (1995). *Mozart: A Life*. New York: Harper Collins.

Sonnenberg. S. M. (2011). Psychoanalysis and United States Research University: Current Trends, *International Journal of Psychoanalysis*, 92 (3): 641–59.

Stekel, W. (1911). Review, *Zentralblatt fur Psychoanalyse und Psychotherapie*, 1: 252–4.

Sterba, R. (1946). Toward the Problem of the Musical Process, *Psychoanalytic Review*, 33: 37–43.

—— (1965). Psychoanalysis and Music, *American Imago*, 22: 96–111.

Thompson, O. (1975). *The International Cyclopedia of Music and Musicians* (Tenth Edition), (ed.) B. Bohle. New York: Dodd, Mead.

Thomson, K. (1977). *The Masonic Thread in Mozart*. London: Lawrence and Wishart.

Ticho, E. (1973). Tichos to Leave Menninger Clinic, *The Menninger Foundation/Employee Publication*, October 5, p. 11.

Ticho, G. (1967). On Self-Analysis, *International Journal of Psychoanalysis*, 68 (2): 308–18.

Twemlow, S. (2009). Commentary on Isaac Tylim's Paper, *International Journal of Applied Psychoanalytic Studies*, 6 (1): 93.

Tylim, I. (2009). Becoming a Psychoanalyst in the Age of Diminishing Expectations: Psychoanalysis in the United Nations, *International Journal of Applied Psychoanalytic Studies*, 6 (1): 94–9.

Verdi, G. (1962/1963) *Otello*. Schirmer Opera Score Editions. Milwaukee, WI: Hal Leonard Corp. (English translation: Walter Ducloux).

— — (1986) *Otello* (orchestral score). New York: Dover Publications, Inc.

— — (1995). *Otello* (DVD), Deutsche Grammophon.

— — (2003). *Otello* (orchestral score), copyright BMG Ricordi S.p.A.-Via Mascagni160 – 00199 Roma.

Wallerstein, R. S. (2011). Psychoanalysis in the University. The Natural Home for Education and Research, *International Journal of Psychoanalysis,* 92 (3): 623–39.

Weinstock, H. (1963). *Donizetti and the World of Opera in Italy, Paris and Vienna in the First Half of the Nineteenth Century.* New York: Pantheon Books.

Wilson, L. (2009). Discussion of Creativity Panel Papers. International Psychoanalytic Association Conference, Chicago, IL (unpublished manuscript).

Wurmser, L. (1981). *The Mask of Shame.* Baltimore, MD: Johns Hopkins University Press.

Zizek, S. (2009). "… I will move the underground": Slavoj Zizek on Udi Aloni's *Forgiveness, International Journal of Applied Psychoanalytic Studies,* 6 (1): 80–3.

Notes

1 Preamble

1 I am indebted to my colleague David Abrams for his scholarship on Max Graf, which informs my own.

2 Case-ette 1

1 *West Side Story* reached a wider audience as a film than as a theatrical work. In fact, there are many versions of the musical that enable it to be performed under a variety of conditions, from strictly orchestral venues to high school performances. The film version is not identical to the Broadway stage production, nor does it utilize the engraved orchestral score. In the film, some of the music is cut and some of the numbers appear in a different order. None of the changes made in the film are reflected in the 1994 engraved orchestral score that was in process at the time of Bernstein's death in 1990. In my discussion of *West Side Story*, where there are differences, I have followed the 1957 original stage version.

2 Around the time of Bernstein's successful debut with the New York Philharmonic Orchestra, with worldwide accolades beginning to accrue, his father, Sam Bernstein, was asked what he thought of his son. In an attempt to deflect a suggestion that he had not supported Leonard's musical talent and ambitions, he replied, "How could I know my son was going to grow up to be Leonard Bernstein?" (Burton, 1994, p. 122).

3 Perhaps the most famous example of the tritone in *West Side Story* (or in any other work) is heard in the first two notes of the song "Maria." I understand from a colleague who is a professor of music theory that this song has become a model for teaching the concept of the tritone to music students.

4 When I speak about music affecting the listener, I am referring implicitly to Western music and the harmonic traditions associated with its history and pervasiveness in our culture. While I believe that music has universal appeal, I do not claim that all music evokes universal responses for everyone regardless of acculturation.

5 Forgiveness does not necessarily have a religious connotation, but can be employed, as Lansky suggests (2007c), as the *outcome* of having worked through splitting and its underlying shame dynamics.

3 Case-ette 2

1 Quotations from the libretto are from the score of *Peter and the Wolf, Opus 67,* Ernst Eulenberg, Ltd., 1985.

4 Case-ette 3

1 The letter *K* that follows the title of Mozart's works refers to the chronological numbering of his compositions by Ludwig von Kochel.
2 Of interest, Bach used the keys of A minor and E minor in some of his most significant keyboard music, e.g., two preludes and fugues, Books I and II, the E Minor English Suite and Partita, the A Minor English Suite and Partita, and the E Minor Toccata.
3 An *appoggiatura* is an ornamental note that embellishes the melody, such as a grace note; it is written smaller than the melodic note.
4 An earlier version of this paper was awarded the Nathan P. Segel Award by the Michigan Psychoanalytic Institute in 2003.

5 Case-ette 4

1 Earlier versions of this paper were presented at the Michigan Psychoanalytic Society, November 17, 2005, and the New Center for Psychoanalysis in Los Angeles, March 2, 2006. A different version, "Psychoanalytic Perspectives on Music: An Intersection on the Oral and Aural Road," was published in *Psychoanalytic Quarterly* (Vol. 77, No. 2, pp. 507–30, April 2008) and dedicated to the memory of my dear friend and colleague, Stuart Feder, M.D.
2 The Bacio music is first heard in the orchestra in Act IV, *without singing,* as Otello enters the bedroom through a secret door, intent on killing his wife. He finds Desdemona asleep, holding her wedding dress. As the Bacio theme is played, he kisses her three times before she awakens.
3 For a comprehensive discussion of tonal centers in the Bacio theme, see David Lawton, 1978, pp. 212–20. It was musicologist Lawton's paper on tonal relationships in *Otello* that stimulated my psychoanalytic understanding of Otello's psychic conflicts. My discussion incorporates a partial summary of his detailed musical analysis.
4 *Otello* page numbers are from the Ricordi orchestral score, 2003 and the G. Schirmer opera score, 1962/1963, as indicated.

6 Case-ette 5

1 Earlier versions of this paper were presented at the New Orleans/Birmingham Psychoanalytic Center on March 23, 2007, and at the American Psychoanalytic Association Spring Meetings, Denver, Colorado, June 23, 2007. This paper was awarded the Nathan P. Segel Award by Michigan Psychoanalytic Institute on June 9, 2007. It was also awarded the 2007 Karl A. Menninger Memorial Award by the American Psychoanalytic Association on January 18, 2008.
2 Page numbers are from the Schirmer score of *Lucia di Lammermoor,* unless otherwise noted.

3 *Bel canto* literally means "beautiful singing" and typically refers to the operatic style of vocal embellishments utilized by Italian composers such as Rossini, Bellini, and Donizetti. Melodic lines are floridly embellished with vocal virtuosity, including trills, high notes, and cadenza-like scale passages. This compositional technique conveyed heightened emotion and was well received by music lovers.

4 I wish to thank musicologist Lawrence Kramer for sharing his thoughts about *bel canto* stylistic conventions as they pertain to multiple functions regarding affect and irony.

5 Page numbers are from the Schirmer score (1898, renewed 1926) of *Lucia di Lammermoor*, unless otherwise noted.

7 Case-ette 6

1 The first version of this paper was written for presentation at the Meetings of the American Psychoanalytic Association in Washington, D.C. June 11, 2010 as a result receiving the Gertrude and Ernst Ticho Award.

Index

A, Ms. (case study) 77–8, 81, 87
Abraham, Karl 17
Abrams, David 15, 16
Abreu Fellows Program 115
adagio/andante model 69
Adorno, Theodor 13
affects: escalation to level of
    instigation 98; fear of 79; Freud
    on 17; isolation of 101; latent
    meanings 29, 76–7; Mozart's,
    reflected in A Minor Piano Sonata
    73, 76; musical expression and
    47, 48, 87; reignited in author by
    9/11 attacks 87–8; revealed
    through music 8, 29, 79–81, 99;
    shame 90
aggression: evoked (in author) by
    juxtaposition of *Otello* and 9/11
    attacks 87–8; link with creativity
    75; link with sexual energy 38,
    48, 112; as part of human nature
    112; *see also* violence
Aitken, Hugh 56
alcohol abuse 101
"also/and" attitude 21
ambiguity: of harmonic
    relationships in *Otello* 83, 87; in
    Peter and the Wolf 55; of "Tristan
    Chord" 7; of the tritone 35, 36,
    37, 38, 45, 46; in *West Side Story*
    33–46, 106
anality: Mozart's 58–9, 75

animals, depiction of 48; *see also Peter
    and the Wolf*
anti-Semitism 10, 12–13
anxiety: evoked by silence 20, 80,
    81; and shame 90
art: Schoenberg on 8
art songs 6
Atkinson, Brooks 33
atonality: anti-Semitism and 10;
    explained 7; Prokofiev apologises
    for 110; *see also* Schoenberg,
    Arnold
audiences: diminishing 113;
    intrapsychic conflicts of 16–17,
    106; reactions to atonality 10
auditory sphere: in relation to music
    of Charles Ives 22–3; role in
    communication between parent
    and child 20–1, 76; studies of
    17–18
aural/oral relationship: convergence
    17–21, 22, 28, 29, 87; divergence
    5–12; intersection 114, 118

B, Mr. (case study) 100–4
Bach, Carl Philipp Emanuel 6
Bach, Johann Sebastian: decline in
    counterpoint style of 63; use of
    tritone 36; "Capriccio on the
    Departure of a Beloved Brother"
    4; "Well-Tempered Clavier"
    64–5